A Place I Didn't Belong

Hope for Adoptive Moms

PAULA FREEMAN

Carpenter's Son Publishing

Published by Carpenter's Son Publishing, Franklin, Tennessee.

Published in association with Larry Carpenter of Christian Book Services, LLC.
www.christianbookservices.com

Printed in the United States of America.

For more information contact:

Hope's Promise
309 Jerry Street, Suite 202
Castle Rock, CO 80104
303-660-0277
www.hopespromise.com
paula@hopespromise.com

Praise for *A Place I Didn't Belong: Hope for Adoptive Moms*

"A hope-filled guide that is sure to encourage and inspire Christian adoptive mothers."

—*Chuck Johnson*
President and CEO
National Council for Adoption

"As much as any expression of love, adoption can weave together both joy and heartache, beauty, and costliness. With candor and hard-won insight, Paula Freeman helps us to hold these seeming opposites together with grace. For those who harbor rose-colored illusions, she offers a frank corrective. For those whose illusions long ago became disillusionment, Freeman offers a pathway home to purpose, compassion, and joy."

—*Jedd Medefind*
President and CE0, Christian Alliance for Orphans
Author, UPENDED

"*A Place I Didn't Belong* is an extraordinary book addressing the often-unspoken and socially-unrecognized wounds of adoptive moms. As an adopted person myself, I know my late mom would have been comforted and encouraged by this articulate, research-based, compassionate book."

—*Sherrie Eldridge*
Author, 20 Things Adopted Kids Wish Their Adoptive Parents Knew
Founder, Jewel Among Jewels Adoption Network, Inc.

"When the challenges of a child's behavior from past hurts set in, our enthusiasm can quickly turn to discouragement. Paula gives us hope-filled, practical tools to remind us we are not alone when we are weary in the journey."

—*Andy Lehman*
Vice President, LifeSong for Orphans

"Paula writes from years of personal experience, both as director of a very successful adoption agency and as an adoptive mom. Parents will find comfort in the knowledge they are not alone in their experiences, and also tools to lead to health and peace within their families."

—Paul Lessard, Senior Pastor
Castle Oaks Covenant Evangelical Church, Castle Rock, Colorado

"Having known Paula for more than twenty years, I thought this book would be good. It isn't good—it is excellent. The learnings are for deep places in our hearts as adoptive parents."

—Tom Wilkens, PhD
Staff Development and Care Director
Church Resource Ministries

"Paula offers moms a safe place to explore and name the hurts they incur as adoptive parents, and permission to heal those wounds. I would definitely recommend it to moms I work with."

—Jennifer Winkelmann, MA, LPC, NCC
Founder and Clinical Director
Inward Bound

"*A Place I Didn't Belong* is a powerful and practical book every person considering adoption needs to read."

—Carol Selander, MA, LPC
Founder/Director
North Cherry Creek Counseling Center, Denver, Colorado

"This book meets a profound need for adoptive mothers. It contributes to the health and promotion of adoptive families like no other. I would wholeheartedly recommend this study to all adoptive families."

—Rachel Harrison, LCPC, NCC
Therapist
Adoptive mom of children with challenges.

"*A Place I Didn't Belong* is powerful. It brings to light the often difficult journey of adoption. The practices throughout the book are excellent for processing through pain in order to find healing, forgiveness, and hope."

    —*Leslie McAninch, MA*

    Counselor

"Having been personally involved in over 3,000 adoptions, I am keenly aware of the need for this book. It is difficult to imagine an adoptive mom who could not relate to and greatly benefit from *A Place I Didn't Belong*. This book works."

    —*Ron Stoddard*

    President, National Christian Adoption Fellowship

    Executive Director, Nightlight Christian Adoption Agency

Table of Contents

PART ONE: A PLACE I DIDN'T BELONG

Foreword by Sherrie Eldridge. 11

Week One: 13
The Journey Begins

Week Two: 19
Expectations and Adoption Realities
    Expectations
    Adoption Realities
    Compromised Beginnings
    The Wounds We Carry

Week Three: 37
Collision
    I Don't Think We're in Kansas Anymore!
    Name it
    Collision Casualties
    Own it

Week Four: 55
A Place I Didn't Belong
    Detours
    Once Upon a Time
    Grieve Our Past Losses
    Embrace Our New Reality

PART TWO: RIGHT INTO HIS ARMS

Week Five: 75
Homeward Bound
    Understanding Our Core Wounds
    Feeling, Nothing More Than Feeling
    Self-Care
    Forgiveness

Week Six: 103
Right into His ARMS
    Allow God to be Your Father
    Rely on God
    Make Room for Sabbath Rest
    Seek Him

Week Seven: 127
Creating Healthy Support Communities
    Building Our House
    Extended Family Members
    The Faith of a Few Close Friends
    Team Building

Week Eight: 153
Glancing Back, Pressing Forward
    Ears to Hear
    A Heart to Understand
    A New Thing
    Reclaiming Hope!

Acknowledgments 167

About the Author 169

Source List 171

Appendix A: God Wants to Adopt You 173

Appendix B: Confidentiality Agreement 177

Appendix C: Feeling Wheel 179

Appendix D: Additional Resources 181

Appendix E: Stepping Stones of Hope 201

PART ONE:
A Place I Didn't Belong

Foreword

When you're hurting, the person you want to share your heartache with is someone who has "been through the fire." That person need not have special words or magic formulas. Instead, there is just something profoundly deep and comforting about their presence.

Paula Freeman, author of *A Place I Didn't Belong*, is one such person. She endured the fires of suffering long before she wrote this book. She knows the heat of disappointed dreams, and the scorching fires of hopelessness after she and her husband adopted.

She's a veteran in the field of adoption on every level.

Not only is she an adoptive mom, she is also the founder and executive director of Hope's Promise, a licensed adoption agency with five Colorado locations.

Now, we are all privileged to be able to read her words in *A Place I Didn't Belong*.

Paula feels burdened for the families who suffer with the same dashed dreams— adoptive parents hopeful that love is all their adopted children will need.

The timeliness of this book is amazing. Such a need for pre- and post-adoption literature from a biblical perspective exists. Evangelicals in the US have awakened to the heart and plight of those touched by adoption, but the resources are scant, at best.

This book targets members of the adoption triad who are usually missing at adoption conferences. Both from within adoption circles and society at large, they are the brunt of romanticism and misunderstanding. "They must be struggling because they adopted." Or, "Their child behaves fine at church. The problem must be with the parenting."

Research studies conducted by Indiana University in 2008 show adoptive parents invest more of themselves and their resources in their children than biological parents. After all, they want to be the best parent possible for this beloved child (children). But, because of self-imposed perfectionism, the bar of acceptance keeps rising.

Adoptive parents are discouraged, and need validation and healing. *A Place I Didn't Belong* provides a practical tool for them to share their stories in a safe environment, with other parents, and also to learn from one who has been through the fires.

Thank you, Paula Freeman, for passing through the fires and assisting fellow parents who will experience many of the same things.

—Sherrie Eldridge
Author, 20 Things Adopted Kids Wish Their Adoptive Parents Knew

WEEK ONE:
The Journey Begins

"So here's what I want you to do, God helping you: Take your every-day, ordinary life your sleeping, eating, going-to-work, and walking-around life and place it before God as an offering."
—Rom 12:1 MSG

"We must come to accept and even honor our creatureliness. The offering of ourselves can only be the offering of our lived experience, because this alone is who we are. And who we are—not who we want to be—is the only offering we have to give."
—Richard Foster

Dear Friend,

When I first felt the Lord's nudge to write, and the idea for this book began to take shape, I remember asking, " . . . but what do you want me to say?" This is what He shared with my heart:

These are my children . . . they are all my children.

I will be with you through joy, pain, and rejection. I know where you are broken, and I know how they have been broken, too. I want them to have families, even imperfect ones. I called Mary to birth and parent My Son against the cultural norms of her time. So I call you. The world may not understand, but I do. Be strong and of good courage.

That's the heartbeat of *A Place I Didn't Belong*—to turn broken hearts and tearstained cheeks to the Father, to exchange lies for truth, and allow Him to right our course. I began my worthy trek of adoption over twenty-five years ago, and eventually found myself at a place I didn't belong. A place marked by fear, disappointment, depression, anger, shame, and self-recrimination. I wonder if you feel beat up, too? A better way—a gentler, kinder way—is available. I invite you to come there with me.

Oh how I wish we could linger, face to face over a cup of tea, and share our joys, sorrows, and all the adjustments we've been required to make as moms since we embarked on our adoption journeys. I would tell you that:

- Adoption didn't turn out the way I thought it would. I suspect that might be true for you.
- I now see life, and experience people, differently.
- I encountered numerous crossroads and crises of faith along the way.
- I'm still in process.
- I cried more tears than could fill an ocean (and suffered the headache afterward).
- I beat myself up, slandered my husband, and yelled at the kids.
- At times I got hung up on behaviors, and forgot to nurture hearts . . . mine and those around me.
- My assumptions about life have changed.
- My view of God has changed.
- My goals scarcely resemble those I held at the start of this journey.
- I entered with noble expectations, and found my wounds.
- Those wounds led me down the path of acceptance, surrender, and rest.
- I don't always practice what I preach, but I wish I did.
- I'm glad I adopted. I still think it's one of God's grandest and most compassionate plans for redeeming the brokenness of our world.
- I finally get it!

This is my offering, to my Lord and the scattered community of adoptive moms who do our best to raise each child God entrusts to us, for however long we have them. I know what shattered dreams and fear for my child's future feel like. I've lived in a war zone with my street address! Maybe you have, too.

My dream to adopt took root as a teenager. I have no earthly clue where it came from. Time and perspective cause me to believe God planted, then nurtured, it through years of motherhood.

Four biological children began our family; three adopted daughters completed it. My husband and I moseyed into adoptive parenthood with many of the same expectations we held for our biological children: we would love them and be loved in return; healthy children would blossom in our loving, Christian family; seasoned parenting skills would prove sufficient for the task; and our marriage would thrive. We were wrong on all counts!

Fear of failure consumed me as expectations withered. I tried harder, prayed louder, and generally wore myself out. Depleted, I slid into the abyss of depression, a most noteworthy failure in my own mind! In retrospect, I view that lonely "pit stop" as one of God's richest blessings. Unmasked, my depression exposed wounds I guarded, ineffective coping tools I refused to abandon, and lies I believed. I confused my self-worth with how my children behaved and "turned out." What a sure-fire recipe for disaster! I'm learning the cross defines my worth and my identity. Lies destroy. That first step out of the pit brought renewed awareness of my role, and acceptance of the limits of my control.

As an adoptive mother and adoption social worker, I've felt incredibly honored as countless moms have shared their stories with me over the years:

- Moms who could no longer deny their child needed help beyond what they could provide.
- Moms angered by the abuse their children suffered at the hands of birth families.
- Moms who despaired of finding the help her child needed.
- Moms whose hearts had grown cold from the rejection, pain, and chaos their adopted son or daughter inflicted.
- Moms who feared for their safety, and the safety of their children.
- Moms who can't remember why they thought adoption might be a good idea in the first place!
- Moms who felt they had wound up in a place they didn't belong.

Several years ago, I attended a friend's wedding. Majestic scenery, a romantic ceremony, and the comfort of a shared history set a high bar for the festivities afterward. As recessional music faded in the background, guests ambled toward the reception hall, casually searching for their assigned dinner seats. My husband and I located our names, sat down, and introduced ourselves to others around our table. As salads arrived, polite conversation focused on how we knew the bride or groom; the entrée provided a backdrop for congenial small talk. By the time dessert appeared, family stories popped into the exchange. I enjoy watching people's varied reactions when they learn we have seven children. When I shared we adopted three of them, however, the conversation abruptly stopped. "Well, that's not natural!" the middle-aged man across the table shot back at me.

"You're right," I agreed. "It's supernatural!"

Perhaps God does place this supernatural desire in our hearts to ensure children are nurtured and cared for. We feel compassion and can't fathom the atrocities that profoundly wound innocent lives. We long to help. Hearts bursting with love compel us to adopt. We dive into paperwork, bare our souls in interviews, and jump through innumerable hoops to bring our child home. We envision happy, active lives with children who love us. So what went wrong?

Many of us who followed this supernatural desire became casualties of the collision between our worthy pursuit and our new reality. We found ourselves in a place we didn't belong, on a journey gone terribly awry. Well intentioned, we opened our hearts and homes only to realize we had no idea what was required.

Now for the good news: we don't have to stay there! It's not a final destination. Our proactive journey over the next few weeks will provide opportunities to take God at His word, to choose to live not in fear, but with a renewed understanding of the enormity of our challenge, and the grace which sustains us. This healing journey is deeply personal, remaining separate from our children and their outcomes. Healing happens in the context of healthy relationships . . . relationships with others, and with our heavenly Father. We'll cultivate both.

This is not a program or another list of "shoulds." You are welcome to join us wherever you are in this process. Proceed at your pace. Use the following pages as a tool, a guided journey with no predetermined outcome, except moving you closer to the healing, peace, and rest you seek. The challenges faced by moms in these stories are real; names and identifying details have been changed to protect confidentiality.

I believe God wants us to live fully and freely, to help build a compassionate community for ourselves and the next generation of adoptive parents. What can happen if communities, churches, and families rally to aid not only vulnerable children, but also to support families who answered the call to adopt? Such change starts with us, with our healing and our voice.

A Place I Didn't Belong validates the sometimes devastating experiences of adoptive parenthood while offering hope, practical coping strategies, and spiritual renewal for the journey ahead. The trajectory of unmet expectations, our children's compromised beginnings, and the wounds we carry into our adoptions conspire to take us to a place we didn't belong. A compassionate look at the causes and behaviors of children with challenges moves us from victim to empowered advocate, and prepares our heart for the Great Exchange, a concept we'll explore later in the book. Insights on spiritual renewal, offered as a cool cup of water from one travel-weary mom to another, help us reclaim hope for our adoption journey. This is not a how-to or a ten-easy-steps-to successful parenting program. It's about real life, real women, and real struggles. It's about relationships and community. It's about reclaiming ourselves as women when adoption dreams shatter. It's about a journey that begins in our mother's heart, and delivers us to the place we do belong . . . right into our Father's arms.

With Great Affection!
Paula

WEEK TWO:
Expectations and Adoption Realities

The disciples came up and asked, "Why do you tell stories?" He replied, "You've been given insight into God's kingdom. You know how it works. Not everybody has this gift, this insight; it hasn't been given to them. Whenever someone has a ready heart for this, the insights and understandings flow freely. But if there is no readiness any trace of receptivity soon disappears. That's why I tell stories: to create readiness, to nudge the people toward receptive insight . . ."
—Matt 13:10-12 MSG

EXPECTATIONS

Expectations permeate our lives. Born of dreams, experience, relationships, or simple observation of how our world works, we rely on predictability from the moment we rise until we fall asleep at night. Unexpected events jar us from autopilot, and force us to examine the gulf between expectation and reality. Sometimes we quickly adjust and move on. Other times we're propelled, kicking and screaming, into a major life transition. For many of us, unmet adoption expectations litter our journey. Dreams shattered, unmet expectations rearranged our lives, and relationships faltered. What happens when expectations collide with reality?

Megan's Story

"I think my adoption journey began at a different place than most," Megan explained. "My dad died when I was a teenager. Our premature daughter died in the wake of my sister-in-law's untimely death. The following year, I delivered a stillborn son. I suffered a lot of loss, and I still wasn't any closer to being a mom!"

Megan longed to love a child. Like many women, being a mom felt more important than being pregnant. Eventually, she and Brett decided to adopt. They chose not to risk another biological loss. "All my losses involved medical disasters," she said. "I believed I could protect my children if I didn't have to carry or birth them; if they came to me by adoption."

Megan and Brett threw themselves into the adoption process. They sought education, evaluated their strengths and weaknesses, and shored up their financial situation. They embraced the challenges of parenthood, and felt wide open to adopting any type of child. "I assumed I would raise my adopted children in much the same way as if I had given birth to them," Megan said. "I expected my children would have the same joys and challenges as other children, and we'd be a regular family. I desperately wanted to love and nurture a child who would, of course, love me back."

Today, Megan and Brett's frenzied lifestyle reflects their commitment to meet the mounting needs of their two active boys, siblings adopted as infants from the foster care system. While they look like normal kids, they aren't. Their birth mother abused drugs and alcohol during her pregnancies. The resulting organic brain damage now consumes their lives. "Like most families with elementary-aged children, our lives are filled with appointments and children's activities. Only we're not playing soccer and going to piano lessons . . . we're keeping therapist, doctor, and counseling appointments. I can't leave my boys with anyone because of raging and erratic behaviors. I don't even try to talk about it with family members or close friends. I know they just won't get it, and I don't have the energy to try to explain anymore. Being the mom of the bad kids makes me sad. At times I just feel hopeless."

Adoption realities eroded Megan's expectations as her sons shed toddlerhood and moved into their pre-school years. Although Megan passionately loves her boys, and has become their greatest advocate, she and Brett redefined successful parenting. "I no longer have the same goals for my children as other moms do," Megan shared. "I'm just hoping to keep my boys out of jail as they grow up." Her sons' inability to understand cause and effect, regulate emotions, and maintain themselves in a normal classroom was compromised before they were born.

Megan and Brett understand their lives will never be "normal"—they don't have a "regular family." This is not how they dreamed of raising children together. Emotional scars now include assaults on their marriage. Personal time and self-care faded from Megan's schedule years ago. "I am so stressed out and focused on my kids, I couldn't even tell you when I got lost in this process," Megan continued. "Even though I know better, finding time to take care of myself just never makes my weekly schedule."

While Megan adjusts her expectations in light of her adoption realities, reclaiming time for personal healing gains importance. "I've done my best to find what help I can for my boys; now I need to take care of me. We've got a long journey ahead of us."

—*Megan and Brett, adoptive parents of two infants from foster care.*

Pam's Story

"Adoption was a natural step for Jay and me to take," Pam said. "Adoption just fit with our values and my medical history. I had difficult pregnancies with our two sons, and my doctor recommended I not have any more children. Jay and I always wanted a large family, and had discussed adopting a child from a different race before we married. After our boys arrived, we realized how much we loved being parents, and it just felt like our family wasn't complete. We knew we didn't need a child to look like us; we had those. We also wanted to help a child who otherwise might not have a family. That made international adoption a logical decision for us."

Confident in their role as parents, Pam and Jay dove into the adoption process. They quickly complied with US and international requirements and were rewarded with the referral of a pre-school-aged girl from Asia. Her photo adorned the refrigerator for months, as their household revolved around her impending arrival. "As part of our preparation, we attended the adoption education class our agency provided," Pam said, "but I had a difficult time connecting the adorable face on my refrigerator with the information about attachment I heard. All that sounded so scary. I never expected any of it would apply to us anyway, since we already had two great kids."

Pam and Jay expected their daughter might struggle with initial adjustments. They also assumed she would eventually thrive in their loving home. As skilled parents with well-adjusted biological children, "it never dawned on us she might not allow herself to receive our love or fit into our family. Boy, were we in for a rude awakening! Nothing prepared me for what the past fifteen years has been like," she said. "I wish I had paid more attention to our adoption training. I wasted valuable time getting the help my daughter needed because I took her behaviors personally; I kept trying to fix me. Thankfully, we did get counseling, worked with an attachment therapist, endured extensive testing, and enrolled her in an alternative high school. As a young adult, she still rejects us and lives a marginalized life outside our home. I feel scared for my daughter's future, but I know I've done all I can for now. This has been a pretty tough road for our whole family."

After years of pain, Pam chose to forgive her daughter and begin her own healing process. "My daughter's rejection, lying, stealing, drama, chaos, and sexual acting out just screamed I had failed as a mom. I don't think that's true anymore, but the years I did believe that took their toll on me."

Pam's journey to her current degree of acceptance proved long and painful. Like Megan, time to heal and address her own issues dropped off the radar until it was nearly too late. "After years of trying to hold my daughter together, I finally sought counseling for myself and admitted I struggled with depression," she shared. "I wasn't surprised. In fact, I felt rather relieved. I knew I'd been dealing with depression for a long time, but I kept thinking I could get my act together by myself. I was wrong. The decision to accept and deal with the underlying causes of my depression put me on the road to healing. I think there are probably lots of other adoptive moms out there who feel like they've been wrenched through a knothole. I'd like to tell them they're not alone, and there is hope!"

—*Pam and Jay, adoptive parents of internationally-born, pre-school-aged child.*

Shattered Dreams

Like many adoptive moms of children with challenges, Megan and Pam often feel isolated from family and friends. Adoption realities shattered their expectations, their dreams, their families, and their hearts. Self-worth disintegrated. Support from church families waned. Friends changed the subject or offered spiritual clichés whenever they dared talk about their reality. Others became judgmental, blaming them for their child's shortcomings. That hurt. What happened to their lives and their dreams?

Megan and Pam each began a noble journey that led to a place they didn't belong: a place filled with fear, isolation, chaos, discord, and self-doubt. They're ready to find their way back, to experience the rest and peace their hearts crave.

Let's begin with a closer look at adoption expectations, adoption realities, and how they interact to set us up for a great collision.

ADOPTION EXPECTATIONS

Unmet or unrealistic adoption expectations usually result from a combination of inadequate education or preparation, personal wounds, societal myths, stereotyping, isolated or sensationalized stories, over-spiritualizing, or a myriad of other, more personal, experiences. They can occur at any point on our adoption journey. When things go awry, it's normal to feel frustrated, and try to get things back on track (like I want or expect them to be!). Once our children are home, however, more drastic fallout, such as anxiety, anger, depression, isolation, or disruption of the adoption may also occur.

God builds families, redeems lives, and provides second chances through adoption. He entrusts children to us as a gift. He also uses them as a magnificent means to help us get over ourselves! Through adoption, children gain families who love, nurture, and prepare them for adulthood. Birth families can choose life for their child, and make an adoption plan when they don't feel prepared to parent. Adoption, at its best, mirrors God's redemptive plan for welcoming us into His family. Most of us thought we signed up for just this part!

The redemptive process, however, may be painful and sacrificial, and provides no guarantees. If adoptive parents receive that message, it's usually tucked in a small disclaimer buried deep within the paperwork (or we're simply not listening for it). We yearn to become happy families and fit inconspicuously into our schools, churches, and communities. Some who come to adoption through infertility feel desperate for a child, any child. Others may adopt because there's room in the family for one more. Either way, our dreams and expectations pave the way.

Expectations and a Mother's Heart

Most adoptions are conceived in a mother's heart—a heart aching to love, nurture, and protect a child. If we've been raised in a "good enough" home, we get it. We know how to love. But, there are some things we expect in return. We expect this long-awaited child to enrich our lives and our marriage. We expect friends and family members will become our greatest support systems. On a spiritual level, we expect to reflect God's image, and pass on a godly heritage. Ultimately, however, when we love, we expect to be loved . . . eventually. Although our mother's hearts are loving and sacrificial, they are not limitless. Few of us, however, realize this at the outset. We can't imagine what it would feel like if our heart grew cold; we certainly can't imagine it would happen because of a child. Rejection never crossed our minds!

We all possess an emotional bank account. If the only activity our account sees is withdrawals, we'll eventually go bankrupt!

ADOPTION REALITIES

Adoptions begin with compromised beginnings—those our child brings, and the personal wounds we carry into the process.

In utero drug and alcohol exposure, malnutrition, abuse, neglect, various kinds of deprivation, poverty, multiple caregivers, maternal mental illness, institutionalization, and the loss of the birth mother, to name a few, rob our children of their potential.

Our adopted child may be our first child, but we're not his or her first mother! Each child has lost at least one mother before we welcomed them into our families. Many have grieved the loss of multiple mothers, each recorded on our child's heart as love going away. Challenging behaviors and other emotional scars announce the wounds these children incurred along the way. These are a typical response to an atypical beginning. Other compromises notwithstanding, a child's broken heart is the starting point in every adoption. Some mend quickly; others never do.

Wounds we carry also infuse our process. The adoption experience itself becomes hurtful to some. Infertility may attack our well-being as women, or suck the life from our marriage. Wounds from hurtful, abusive backgrounds lie hidden, ready to erupt in emotionally-charged situations. Poorly-managed past issues often manifest themselves in destructive ways during the stress of an adoption.

The trajectory of our unmet expectations, our children's compromised beginnings, and the wounds we carry into our adoptions conspire to take us to a place we didn't belong. Understanding how we got here is the first step toward healing.

DAILY SESSIONS: WEEK TWO

For sighing comes to me instead of food;
my groans pour out like water.
What I feared has come upon me;
what I dreaded has happened to me.
I have no peace, no quietness;
I have no rest, but only turmoil.
—Job 3:24-26

SOME THOUGHTS BEFORE YOU BEGIN:

- Offer yourself to the Lord each day . . . just the way you are!

- Set aside time to think about and record your answers to each day's questions.

- Ask God to quiet your heart and mind; invite Him into your process. He is the only one who truly knows you, your child, your family, and your story.

- Notice and make note of your feelings. Give yourself permission to feel the wide range of emotions certain to surface.

- Be honest . . . no over-spiritualizing, criticism, or judgment allowed.

- Give God permission to love you!

- There is no right or wrong answer. Dispense with "shoulds."

- Be gentle with yourself!

DAY ONE:

Expectations

*Trust in the LORD with all your heart and lean not
on your own understanding; in all your ways acknowledge him,
and he will make your paths straight.*
—Proverbs 3:5-6

BEFORE YOU BEGIN:

- Pray. Ask God to quiet your mind and help you be receptive to His voice.
- Determine to be gut-level honest in your responses.
- Commit yourself to the Lord's healing process for you.

QUESTIONS:

1. What were your pre-adoption expectations? Include expectations for the adoption process, the professionals who helped you, what you expected of your spouse, as well as your personal dreams.

2. Where did those expectations come from (dreams, fears, other people's experiences, media, faith, etc.)?

3. As a mother-to-be, what were the dreams of your heart?

NOTICING:

What physical reactions and feelings did you notice?

PRAYER:

Thank You, Father, for knowing all my expectations. Help me remember them. I trust You and not my own understanding on this journey. Give me courage to continue; to choose Your path back.

DAY TWO:
Adoption Realities

No one will be able to stand up against you all the days
of your life. As I was with Moses, so I will be with you;
I will never leave you nor forsake you.
Have I not commanded you? Be strong and courageous.
Do not be terrified; do not be discouraged, for the LORD
your God will be with you wherever you go.
—Joshua 1:5-9

BEFORE YOU BEGIN:

- Pray. Ask God to quiet your mind and help you be receptive to His voice.
- Determine to be gut-level honest in your responses.
- Commit yourself to the Lord's healing process for you.

QUESTIONS:

1. Describe your current adoption reality (behaviors of your challenging children; effects on you, your marriage, and siblings; life adjustments you've made; etc.).

2. Take a few minutes to remember who you were before you began the adoption process. Write a letter to yourself—something you'd like to tell your pre-adoptive self. (Use additional paper if you need more room.)

NOTICING:

What physical reactions and feelings did you notice?

PRAYER:

Thank You, Father, for promising never to leave or forsake me. I need Your strength and courage.

DAY THREE:
Compromised Beginnings

For you created my inmost being;
you knit me together in my mother's womb.
I praise you because I am fearfully and wonderfully made;
your works are wonderful,
I know that full well.
My frame was not hidden from you
when I was made in the secret place.
When I was woven together in the depths of the earth,
your eyes saw my unformed body.
All the days ordained for me
were written in your book
before one of them came to be.
—Psalm 139:13-16

BEFORE YOU BEGIN:

- Pray. Ask God to quiet your mind and help you be receptive to His voice.
- Determine to be gut-level honest in your responses.
- Commit yourself to the Lord's healing process for you.

A FIVE-STORY FALL

We don't expect a person who falls from a fifth-story window to walk away unscathed; they'd be lucky to survive! As bystanders, we might help mitigate the damage. Medical training and a willingness to get involved would help. I believe it's fair to assume a five-story fall survivor will never be the same. They may not walk again. If they do, there would certainly be a noticeable limp. They would also sustain other wounds, some visible and some invisible. We don't expect them, or their caregivers, to look and act like they hadn't endured such a tragedy.

Many of our children have survived such falls emotionally, spiritually, mentally, or physically. As parents, our responsibility is to mitigate the damage, and help them achieve their greatest post-fall potential. Some have suffered irreparable harm from biological parents; others experienced damage due to drug and alcohol abuse before they were born, or bear institutional scars. All have severed relationships with at least one mother.

The farther we move away from God's plan, the more drastic the consequences can become. I frequently wonder what God's original design was for our children. Did it grieve His heart when their mom drank alcohol or did drugs in the midst of their creation? Through no fault of their own, some children must endure lifelong consequences similar to surviving a five-story fall. Expectations need adjustment (ours and those of the support community we rely upon). We must prepare for battle: spiritual battle. We need to applaud those families who undertake raising these children. We can't do that well without understanding there are significant differences. Broken hearts, broken bodies, and broken spirits don't fit into the same molds our healthy children do. Many rage. Some withdraw. All feel abandoned.

QUESTIONS:

1. Describe your child's "five-story fall":

   a. In what way or ways was your child compromised before they came into your family? (For ideas, look at the checklist in Question Two.)

   b. How would you describe their early wounds? How have those manifested themselves over time?

   c. What challenging behaviors related to these wounds does your child exhibit?

2. Check all that apply to your child. This can be either their history before they arrived, or their behaviors and diagnoses since being in your family.

___ History of abuse and neglect
___ Victim of sexual abuse
___ Sexual abuse perpetrator
___ Multiple caregivers
___ Abandoned
___ Institutionalized
___ Adopted from a county child welfare system
___ Adopted internationally
___ History of malnutrition
___ Sensory integration disorder
___ Involvement with juvenile justice system
___ Steals from friends and/or family member
___ Steals from stores, etc.
___ Does poorly in school
___ Has trouble making friends
___ Has trouble keeping friends
___ Attention deficit disorder
___ Attention deficit hyperactivity disorder
___ Enrolled in special education classes
___ Attachment disorder
___ On medication to control behavior
___ Autism spectrum disorder

___ Bipolar disorder
___ Poor impulse control
___ Organic brain damage
___ Brain chemistry changes
___ Developmental delays
___ Emotional disregulation
___ Physical disability
___ Parent(s) died
___ Cognitive disability
___ Hypervigilant
___ IQ below 70
___ Runs away
___ Depression
___ Conduct disorder
___ Product of incest
___ Lies
___ Sexual acting out
___ Sexually active
___ Rages
___ Witnessed war atrocities
___ Victim of ritual abuse
___ Other: _____

3. How many items checked are, or could be, adoption related?

4. Identify and name the feelings you have as you read back through this list. Use the Feeling Wheel in Appendix C as needed.

5. Rewrite Psalm 139:13-16 in the space below, and exchange your son or daughter's name for the personal references in the Psalm (for example, For you created Tommy's inmost being, you created him in his mother's womb).

NOTICING:

What physical reactions and feelings did you notice?

PRAYER:

Father, sometimes I don't understand Your ways. But I trust You. What do You want me to know about my child? Help me to listen to Your heart.

DAY FOUR:
The Wounds We Carry

For I am poor and needy,
and my heart is wounded within me.
—Psalm 109:22

He heals the brokenhearted and binds up their wounds.
—Psalm 147:3

BEFORE YOU BEGIN:

- Pray. Ask God to quiet your mind and help you be receptive to His voice.
- Determine to be gut-level honest in your responses.
- Commit yourself to the Lord's healing process for you.

Our children are not the only ones who enter this adoption arrangement with compromised beginnings. All of us bring personal wounds into our adoptions; some become further wounded in the process.

Today's time may challenge you. Please be kind to yourself, honest in your evaluation, and willing to forgive yourself and others as you forge ahead.

We have all sinned, and we have all been sinned against. We are the walking wounded! The intent of this re-visitation to those wounded places is not to cast blame or remind us of our shame, but rather to help us understand the contribution our wounds bring to our relationships and our families.

QUESTIONS:

1. What are some of the emotional wounds or baggage you carry? Where did they come from?

2. How would you describe one of your greatest fears? As you reflect back on your life, where do you think this fear first took root?

3. How has your challenging child exploited or manipulated these wounds or fears?

NOTICING:

What physical reactions and feelings did you notice?

PRAYER:

Write a prayer to God about your experience of this week's process.

WEEKLY SUMMARY AND MEETING

Insights, Thoughts, Comments, and Questions from Reading and Daily Exercises:

How God met me this week:

Support Group Meeting Notes:

WEEK THREE:
Collision

*"I am falling apart at the seams, and feel like my soul
is leaking out all over the place. I feel like I've lived a
thousand years in the last few weeks."*
—Anonymous adoptive mother

COLLISION CASUALTIES

Collisions happen when we recognize and admit the realities of our adoption have fallen drastically short of our expectations, and threaten to unravel our very souls. We no longer believe our own excuses for our child's behavior or limitations. Denial requires more energy than we have to spend. Fear consumes our thoughts, and joy becomes a foreign language. Although the face in the mirror looks vaguely familiar, we don't recognize the woman we've become. We spend more time in the principal's office, and make excuses for not meeting friends for coffee. We know love is not enough, but we don't have a clue what is. We can't find resources to help our children; we don't even know where to begin. We feel inadequate and ineffective. Some hearts grow cold and unforgiving toward the child who has seemingly ruined our family. Marriages suffer; some fail. Other children in our homes become wounded in the process. Casualties abound as families boldly answer God's call to care for the least of these, never anticipating the toll of such faithfulness on their lives.

Raina's Story

"Our collision has been moment to moment, almost from the start," Raina explained. "We have experienced a whirlwind of issues, both medical and behavioral, which led to financial struggles. They are truly non-stop. We are four years into this journey and have not had more than a month without a new issue surfacing. My collision has been a collision with the reality of the endurance required here."

Raina knew she had the capacity to deeply love a child; the idea of parenting felt almost magical. She grew up in a loving family, excelled in school, and enjoys the respect of clients and colleagues in her chosen career. Although she understood she and Carlos would encounter challenges along the way, she felt ready for adoptive motherhood. Nothing, however, prepared her for the devastation her son's five-story fall brought into her own young family.

"Samuel quite literally crashed into this world," she said. A violent conception, combined with his birth mother's substance abuse and lack of prenatal care, united to evict him from the womb eight weeks early. "I sometimes wonder how his little body and mind responded to the chemical cocktails he was exposed to."

Raina and Carlos first met their son in the hospital as he was suffering the painful effects of drug withdrawal. His birth mother never held him, and left the hospital against medical advice. "He was alone in the nursery, with strangers and an addiction," Raina said. "The nurses believed that once he was weaned off the drugs, he would be fine. I think we believed that, too . . . or at least hoped it would be true. Those beliefs seem crazy to me now!"

Raina added detective and sleuth to her all-consuming job description. "I find myself constantly searching for answers because nothing really fits." Samuel's extensive medical history includes diagnosed and undiagnosed illnesses. While he appears to suffer from attention deficit hyperactivity disorder (ADHD), his bent toward movement and destruction points to something more complex.

Like many adoptive moms of children with challenges, Raina strives to make sense of her collision. "Brokenness is my adoption reality. My son's story begins with brokenness: his and his birth mother's. Then he joined with our infertility-inflicted broken-ness. We're doing our best to make it work and heal."

Raina admits love is not enough to heal her son. The wounds and disabilities he sustained require serious intervention. "I am the bystander of my son's five-story fall. I see his injuries, but I don't have the tools to heal him, or even know how to find those who do. And, my five-story fall is the wounding I feel every time I am not able to help him."

—*Raina and Carlos, adoptive parents of an infant through an agency adoption.*

Kristy's Story

Kristy and Joe simply wanted to love another child. "Becca was wonderful for many years," Kristy said. "We home schooled her along with our other children to help with attachment. We realized she suffered with some learning disabilities, but had no idea she would never overcome them. I guess you could say our journey through unmet expectations was more like an erosion than a collision . . . until it arrived!"

Depression and isolation from her family accompanied the onset of Becca's adolescence. "About that time we also learned she had been prenatally exposed to alcohol. After years of testing and consulting with various professionals, she was eventually diagnosed with fetal alcohol spectrum disorder (FASD). We learned FASD often manifests itself in a 'ceiling' of development, social maturity, judgment, and learning. So, until she hit this ceiling, we had no idea how severe her problems really were," Kristy explained.

Kristy and Joe anguish over how to help their teenage daughter. She drives, but can't keep a job because of her inability to learn new skills. Adrift in a world of her own making, Becca grows more non-communicative with family members while "stalking" friends through texting, social networking sites, and phone calls. Her lack of judgment causes friends to shun her. She has become sexually active and sneaks out at night. "Joe and I believe it's our responsibility to keep her safe from the world, and the world safe from her. But I just don't know how we can continue to do that," said Kristy.

The loss of a meaningful parent-child relationship is not the only casualty of Kristy and Joe's adoption. "We have also lost many friends over this. People in our church think we have done something horrible. Why else would Becca have so many problems? She is private about her FASD, so we don't discuss it much. When we do, people either don't believe us, or they don't understand, and say we are hiding behind it and not taking responsibility for our daughter's behavior like we should," added Kristy.

Becca is a beautiful young woman who doesn't look disabled. Her five-story fall resulted in an invisible disability that challenges her and other family members. While Becca won't graduate college, and may not be self-sufficient as an adult, she does have areas of strength Joe and Kristy try to cultivate. "We capitalize on these areas to help her feel successful in a world where she does not fit well," Kristy explained, "but we really don't know what to do next. I'm exhausted, wounded by family and friends, and fearful for Becca's future."

—*Kristy and Joe, adoptive parents of a toddler from Asia.*

COLLISION CAUSES

Adoption collisions are as unique and complex as the families in which they occur. Most of us could probably find several applicable to our situation. We rarely have just one; multiple, fatal linkages often exhaust our ability to cope. Following are some of the more common contributing factors:

- Lack of adoption education and training (or we think the training won't apply to us).
- Unrealistic expectations.
- Personal wounds and emotional baggage left unattended before we adopt.
- Unknown or undiagnosed physical or mental health issues in the child.
- Organic brain damage in the child.
- Adopting to meet our needs, rather than focusing on the needs of the child.
- A child's broken heart impeding the ability to trust or form healthy attachments.
- Adoptive mothers become a child's primary target.
- Rigid parenting styles and inflexible parenting methods.
- Adoptive parents' high level of need to control.
- Measuring our self-worth by the behavior and outcome of our children.
- Rejection.
- Lack of meaningful support from family and friends.
- Legalistic religious beliefs.
- Holding a high value on "looking good."
- Predisposition to needing to "fix" others.
- Desperate to become parents.
- Trying to do it all, without realizing how much time this child will take.

- Perfectionist tendencies, and
- Other: Add yours here!

That's a pretty tough list to read. Somehow, it's difficult to not throw value judgments into the mix and beat ourselves up. Remember, we agreed to be gentle with ourselves. None of us have done this perfectly, but seldom are the challenges our children face our fault. We're the "clean-up" crew of their five-story fall. Now, read through the list again, this time with gentleness, compassion, and an open mind . . . but no value judgments!

Although difficult, collisions are seldom fatal. The longer we fail to acknowledge them, however, the more damage produced. Denial also robs us of valuable time. Regardless of where we are in the process, hope and practical help are available to mitigate the damage; more on that in following chapters. For now, let's take some time to examine our own collision and its potential impact.

DAILY SESSIONS: WEEK THREE

"For I know the plans I have for you," declares the LORD, "plans to prosper you and not to harm you, plans to give you hope and a future. Then you will call upon me and come and pray to me, and I will listen to you. You will seek me and find me when you seek me with all your heart. I will be found by you," declares the LORD, "and will bring you back from captivity. I will gather you from all the nations and places where I have banished you," declares the LORD, "and will bring you back to the place from which I carried you into exile."
—Jeremiah 29:11-14

SOME THOUGHTS BEFORE YOU BEGIN:

- Offer yourself to the Lord each day . . . just the way you are!

- Set aside time to think about and record your answers to each day's questions.

- Ask God to quiet your heart and mind; invite Him into your process. He is the only one who truly knows you, your child, your family, and your story.

- Notice and make note of your feelings. Give yourself permission to feel the wide range of emotions certain to surface.

- Be honest . . . no over-spiritualizing, criticism, or judgment allowed.

- Give God permission to love you!

- There is no right or wrong answer. Dispense with "shoulds."

- Be gentle with yourself!

DAY ONE:

"I Don't Think We're in Kansas Anymore . . ."

The LORD is a refuge for the oppressed,
a stronghold in times of trouble.
Those who know your name will trust in you,
for you, LORD, have never forsaken those who seek you.
—Psalm 9:9-10

BEFORE YOU BEGIN:

- Pray. Ask God to quiet your mind and help you be receptive to His voice.
- Determine to be gut-level honest in your responses.
- Commit yourself to the Lord's healing process for you.

QUESTIONS:

1. When did you first suspect all was not well with your adoption? Describe how you responded to those suspicions. How did you feel? Who did you tell? Who did you deliberately not tell? What did you do to try and fix the situation? What did you think about yourself as a mother?

2. What excuses did you use for your child's behavior? When did you stop believing those excuses?

3. Describe your "denial" process and tools. Tools include coping strategies such as denial, minimizing, excusing behaviors, blaming others, over-spiritualizing, extreme busyness, or simply rationalizing these behaviors. Be honest here, but no judgments!

NOTICING:

What physical reactions and feelings did you notice?

PRAYER:

Oh Father, thank You for knowing my heart and the ways I have coped with this disappointment. Thank You for being my refuge. I trust You as my stronghold.

DAY TWO:

Name It

"At the worst point, I would describe our collision as total chaos. Our home felt as though Satan himself had moved in. I feared for our daughter's safety as well as our own; at one point she stated she would kill us in our sleep. Only God could fix this, and I prayed like I never prayed before—and I still pray daily. My life is always chaotic. That is our new reality, like it or not. We have to rely on God for daily strength. If I'm not laughing, I am crying. This is not what I wanted, but that's our life right now. Hard."
—J., Adoptive mother of teenage daughter adopted at birth.

"Our collision was more like a slow-motion accident—it was not a quick and painful hit, but a long, drawn-out incident. We didn't have our 'aha' moment that something was truly wrong for many years. We questioned ourselves more than we questioned our child's behavior, even though we had three 'successful' toddlers already. I felt if only I would do something different, she would be OK. Not until our marriage was severely suffering, and I was the one tanking it, did we seek help. I felt we had failed—we just did not know how to be good parents anymore."
—N., Adoptive mother of a teenage daughter adopted as a toddler.

BEFORE YOU BEGIN:

- Pray. Ask God to quiet your mind and help you be receptive to His voice.
- Determine to be gut-level honest in your responses.
- Commit yourself to the Lord's healing process for you.

QUESTIONS:

1. Here's how others have described their experience:

Deidre: *I felt depressed and bummed out. I tried to give someone a chance at life, and it backfired, putting even more strain on our marriage, and pitting us against each other. This whole situation exposed and exploited our flaws.*

Tiffany: *I think the collision was subtle, yet massive. About three years ago, I finally realized you can't erase trauma just with good parenting—and what is good parenting, anyway? When society says good kids equal good parents, it's hard to be real. I didn't really face the full scope of difficulties my kids face now, and will face in their futures, until I was in an adoption community giving me permission to struggle without judgment.*

Kayla: *For years, I just tried harder to be the good mom I once thought I was. I pulled back from friendships and family members. My decade long erosion, marked by ineffective coping strategies, catapulted me into my major collision—depression.*

Whom do you most identify with, and why?

2. Would you describe your experience as collision or erosion? Erosion is a growing awareness and acknowledgement things are not, and have not been, well. Name your collision, and explain it below:

3. Is your child's challenge or disability visible or invisible? Perhaps it is both. Describe your child's challenges below. How has that affected your collision?

NOTICING:

What physical reactions and feelings did you notice?

PRAYER:

Father, thank You for the courage to revisit the disappointment and fear of my unmet expectations. Please meet me here and help me hear Your voice. I need You to sing a love song over me. I'm ready to listen.

DAY THREE:

Collision Casualties

I have set the LORD always before me.
Because he is at my right hand,
I will not be shaken.
—Psalm 16:8

BEFORE YOU BEGIN:

- Pray. Ask God to quiet your mind and help you be receptive to His voice.
- Determine to be gut-level honest in your responses.
- Commit yourself to the Lord's healing process for you.

QUESTIONS:

1. Collisions happen when we recognize and admit that the realities of our adoption have fallen drastically short of our expectations, and now threaten to unravel our very souls. Go back to the section "Collision Casualties" at the beginning of this chapter. Highlight every statement applicable to you. Identify and write your thoughts and feelings here:

2. What other losses do you associate with your adoption collision? These could be marriages, careers, self-esteem, friendships, etc.

3. List everyone your adoption collision has impacted.

NOTICING:

What physical reactions and feelings did you notice?

PRAYER:

Thank You, Father, for being unafraid of the enormity of my collision. You know it all, even those pieces I'm afraid to acknowledge, or don't realize exist. Thank You for Your kind and gentle ways—even when I feel my heart break all over again.

DAY FOUR:

Own It

We were under great pressure, far beyond our ability to endure, so that we despaired even of life. Indeed, in our hearts we felt the sentence of death. But this happened that we might not rely on ourselves but on God, who raises the dead . . . On him we have set our hope that he will continue to deliver us, as you help us by your prayers.
—2 Corinthians 1:8b-11

"We cannot control all that happens to us, but we can control how we choose to respond to what happens to us."
—John Baker, *Life's Healing Choices*

BEFORE YOU BEGIN:

- Pray. Ask God to quiet your mind and help you be receptive to His voice.
- Determine to be gut-level honest in your responses.
- Commit yourself to the Lord's healing process for you.

QUESTIONS:

Today's topic may be challenging, but it will get easier. In fact, this may be some of the most liberating work we do! Although we may believe it's our job to hold our families together, or carry the weight of our child's five-story fall, we have also contributed to this situation in some way. Perhaps we denied, excused, self-medicated, or blamed others. Maybe we tried harder, worked more, or isolated ourselves and our families. Whatever it is, we need to identify and own our part in the story in order to experience the healing our hearts desire. You are dearly loved. No one will find blame or condemnation here. The truth will set you free.

Read back over the personal collision accounts from Day Two. None of these precious women were to blame for the behaviors of their challenging child. Yet, each of them carried personal wounds, life experiences, or adoption expectations which affected their perception of the challenges they endured. Take a moment to review your collision story before proceeding.

1. With a spirit of gentle objectivity, identify your contribution to your adoption collision.

2. Stop. Put this book down. Relax, take a deep breath, and be present with the Lord. Maybe you would like to pray and ask God's forgiveness for your role in creating the present situation (1 John 1:8-9). Is He inviting you to receive and experience His forgiveness? Perhaps He is affirming His choice of you as your child's mom. Write a prayer of response below:

Gina's Epiphany

"I had to come to the end of myself before I was ready to listen to the Lord," Gina shared. "The events of that long-ago afternoon feel as real to me today as they did then!"

Gina collapsed into her favorite chair; exhaustion seeped from every pore. The day's challenges had exceeded her capacity, and it was only noon! The edge loomed. She felt it threaten to engulf her as she sought a moment of refuge during her chaotic day. "I knew I had reached my breaking point," she shared. "None of this was turning out like I thought it would. Something was terribly wrong with my son. I had also begun to believe I was a horrible mother! That afternoon, while my son napped, I cried out to God, 'I can't do this!'"

"I know," came the gentle reply. "You can't do this without Me; it's Me you need to count on, not yourself."

3. Most of us have earned our "A" for effort. Yet peace, rest, and acceptance may elude us. As we close out today's time, write a love letter of forgiveness, release, or permission to yourself:

NOTICING:

What physical reactions and feelings did you notice?

PRAYER:

Father, You know I have been under great pressure that feels far beyond my ability to endure. By Your grace, help me rely on You and not on my own strength.

WEEKLY SUMMARY AND MEETING

Insights, Thoughts, Comments, and Questions from Reading and Daily Exercises:

How God met me this week:

Support Group Meeting Notes:

WEEK FOUR:
A Place I Didn't Belong

*"I walked a long but worthy road that led
to a place where I didn't belong."*
—Andrew Krivak, *A Long Retreat: In Search of a Religious Life*

Andrew Krivak, a modern day Jesuit priest, chronicles his spiritual journey in a memoir entitled *A Long Retreat: In Search of a Religious Life*. He recounts how, shortly before he took his final vows, he decided to leave the priesthood to marry and raise a family. Later, when asked to explain his decision to a questioning friend, he simply said, "I walked a long but worthy road that led to a place where I didn't belong." Wow! How many of us set off on our adoption journey filled with hope we'd finally become a mom, or a sense of God's calling as, we welcomed one more into our family? We each began with hopes, dreams, and more love than we knew what to do with, only to one day admit this long but worthy road led to a place we didn't belong.

Leah's Story

"I had it all figured out—my life plan, that is," Leah said. "I grew up in a family who highly valued education. My dad was a pastor, and my mom a teacher. I loved being

Mrs. Johnson's daughter, so I guess I just set about recreating that life for myself. I became a teacher, and then married a man just like my dad . . . only he's a teacher, too. I had this great picture of our future. I'd get pregnant, eat chocolate, and Ken would rub my feet. Once our kids arrived, they'd just step in and play the role—our kids would go to our school, participate in sports, and, of course, be brilliant. They'd love having their parents teach at their school and, in general, we would live happily ever after. Everything about that scenario so did not happen, except the committed husband part!"

Like many adoptive moms who entered this adoption world through infertility, Leah became all too familiar with detours, alternate routes, and grief. Determination fueled her efforts to put her life back on track. "All around me, friends became pregnant and entered this strange society of motherhood. I clearly didn't belong. I hated baby showers. They just reminded me of what I didn't have and desperately wanted . . . a baby!"

As pregnancy continued to elude Leah and Ken, they veered onto detour number one, medical testing. The diagnosis of male factor infertility quickly shattered their dreams, eroded their hopes, and undermined their marriage. "I've endured a pretty long grief process," Leah explained. "I can't share my struggle with Ken without sounding like I blame him. Actually, I think I've just been afraid of the grief. Everything keeps piling up on me. I can't seem to work hard enough, or run fast enough, to get out from under it. I'm drowning. I have this picture of myself struggling to balance all my baggage, pieces of varying size and weight. I'm lost, invisible under the pile. I don't dare move a piece, or let someone help me carry the load, because I'm afraid it will all come crashing down on me." Leah's life spiraled out of control as she and Ken encountered additional detours on the road to parenthood.

Infertility diagnosis in hand, and determined to keep her grief at bay, Leah entered the adoption process convinced she would now return to her life plan and join the coveted motherhood club. She and Ken submitted mounds of paperwork, opened their wounds for strangers to inspect, attended adoption training classes, and tried to educate their families about this new world they would also now enter. The gap between Leah's plans and her reality widened exponentially. "We adopted three kids in six years. What were we thinking? Our kids are racially diverse, and come from such different backgrounds. All three have suffered five-story falls. Managing the relationships with all the birth families feels like a full-time job," Leah shared, "and the kids didn't exactly step right in and play their assigned roles! Meaning I can't play my imagined role, either. Yeah, I guess I did end up at a place I didn't belong. That's been a hard one for me to admit. I know God has a plan for me and my family, probably tucked somewhere in this baggage I'm juggling. I don't even know how to start unpacking it."

—Ken and Leah, adoptive parents of three children adopted as infants through agency adoptions.

Natalie's Story

A familiar voice, with an unexpected message, greeted Natalie on the phone. She and David had begun the process to adopt a little girl from Asia, and were waiting for a referral. What did her social worker just say about a two-year-old little girl who lived right here? Natalie fought through confusion to focus on the conversation. "Our birth parent counselor has been meeting with a young mom who's involved with drugs, and on the verge of losing custody of her daughter. This mom wants to consider an adoption plan, and we thought of you. Would you be interested in considering this situation?"

That first conversation now feels surreal. "I thought it was the beginning of a lovely journey into the joys of mothering a daughter. As the mother of three biological sons, I longed for a daughter . . . the hair, the long chats together, and the mother-daughter bond," said Natalie. "All that was part of the dream, as we continued to build our family through adoption."

Some dreams die hard. "We did proceed with the adoption. We experienced the traditional honeymoon period before things went south. We had issues and more issues, but I kept thinking if I tried harder, or loved more, or did something different, then everything would fall into place. I lived many years denying my dream would never come true. I grew frustrated and angry; I hardened my heart. I built walls around my heart, and soon we lived in a two-walled home—my heart, and my child's heart. I thought I would finally be safe, and no longer wounded by the stuff going on around me," said Natalie

"Looking back, I recognize depression had a deep and violent hold on me, to the extent that one Christmas I thought just disappearing into the water and never coming back, like Shakespeare's Ophelia, would be a welcome and refreshing break from the tyranny of this life. I was in a place I didn't belong, but I still couldn't see the truth of the situation. The clouds of self-doubt and despair were too thick and heavy."

As Natalie continued to build emotional walls, cracks appeared in her marriage. "That was my wake-up call," she continued, "I realized we were now on sacred ground, and it felt pretty shaky."

She and David sought counseling for themselves, and outside resources for their daughter. They admitted the challenges at home now exceeded their capacity to deal with on their own. "Counseling brought me back to the reality of my specialness in Christ, and that my child had serious problems I would not be able to fix. My depression began to fade in light of the truth. I did finally grieve the loss of my imagined relationship, but it happened over time. Grieving was a pretty important piece of my healing process."

Natalie also learned how to embrace her new reality. "I now understand that my relationship with my daughter will be based on brokenness—hers and mine. This changes my expectations of her. I'm learning I can live a life that does not need to be wrapped up in her distorted perspective of life. On a practical level, David and I have learned to decentralize her issues instead of making them the centerpiece of the family. That's been great for our marriage, and good for the boys. I can care without having to own the problem, accepting my child might not ever change. I'm growing in my ability to accept my child may not ever be able to accept or give love in the manner I hoped for. I'm beginning to dream new dreams, and reclaim some hope for our journey."

—*David and Natalie, adoptive parents of a two-year-old girl through an agency adoption.*

ADOPTION DETOURS

Detours litter the adoption landscape. If you find yourself in a place you don't belong, or have ever been there, take heart. This isn't a final destination! We can get back on course. A closer look at the detours we've encountered, and the tolls they've extracted, will help us recognize the need to grieve our losses and embrace our new reality.

Alternate Routes Required

Many of us created life plans to include marriage and children. For reasons frequently outside of our control, one or both of those might have been derailed. Detours through infertility treatments assault our emotional well-being and bank accounts. Time ticks on. Allowing ourselves necessary time to grieve the profound loss of not having a biological child devours more time and energy. Not grieving, however, demands a greater toll.

Adoption is an alternate route to parenthood filled with additional detours. We dole out more emotion, energy, money, and time. Meanwhile, we keep spinning life's normal wheels, such as jobs, school, church activities, and cultivating relationships of all kinds.

We now admit our private world diverges from those around us who stumble effortlessly into parenthood. Empty arms ache to hold a child. When can we resume our plan?

How our children arrive in our families propels us through further detours. We feel directionally challenged and lost. Perhaps we step out of the normal rhythms of life to travel to our child's birth country, an adventure dragging more emotion, energy, money, and time from us. If our children come from foster care, *vroom!* We skid into another world filled with case workers, different terminology, and unpredictable timelines. Here, we may encounter the first clue our child suffered a five-story fall, the ramifications of which we can't begin to imagine. This detour extracts further payment of emotion, energy, and time. Parents matched with a birth mother, who adopt their child as an infant, detour through landscapes of legal risk, and relational issues with the birth family. The toll extracted? You got it: emotion, energy, money, and time.

We successfully navigate most adoption detours; we adjust and move on. Although some detours prove isolating, expensive, and emotionally draining, hope endures. We still expect to join the ranks of delighted parents everywhere. The illusion we can regain control of our life plan still appears attainable. We can't imagine we'll be forced to take an alternate route for the rest of our lives!

The Power of a Broken Heart

Every adoption begins with a child's broken heart. Regardless of the quality of the in utero environment, mommies and babies bond with one another. Separation at birth, or anytime during childhood, severs this bond, creating one, and probably two, broken hearts.

Think back to significant losses in your life, or in the lives of a close friend or loved one. When, for example, do you think a woman "gets over" the loss of a child or her husband? Never! As adults, these women have fully-developed brains. They understand bad things happen to good people. They cultivate support networks. Perhaps their faith community, friends, and family rally to their side. Still, such loss is staggering in magnitude; it's traumatic! A typical response to loss, in addition to grief, is to establish defenses meant to decrease the likelihood of ever again sustaining such a blow. Women of child-bearing age who have lost multiple children frequently choose sterilization. They don't believe they could survive another such loss. This is a normal response to a traumatic event.

How much more, then, would a child suffer the loss of his or her only bond? Babies and children also have defense mechanisms for emotional loss. They intuitively believe it would kill them if they lost another mother, so they may try to ensure they never have another mother. They don't understand relinquishment, the best interests of the child standard, or legal adoptions. They can insulate and protect their broken hearts. This response often results in children who refuse to give and receive love, do it on their terms, or reject the limits of our control as parents. They will go to extraordinary lengths to stay in charge. No more change or sudden losses for them! They get stuck in survival mode just when we're ready to resume our happily-ever-after journey. The good-enough love we're bursting to give, expecting our child will eventually return, gets short-circuited by a broken heart.

Mom as Target

Adoptive moms come in all shapes, colors, and sizes, but we all have one thing in common. We wear a bull's-eye on our heart! Once the bond between a child and biological mother is broken, some children determine to protect themselves from further trauma at all costs. Deep in their soul, they resolve not to have another mom (they still need a maid, cook, and chauffeur; they just won't allow emotional intimacy or control). Mom then becomes the target of her child's rejection, because she represents the greatest threat to the child's defenses. Although such rejection frequently attacks our self-worth as moms, it's a positional rejection, not a personal one.

Abandonment is a typical, yet often unconscious, fear for an adopted person; this may be their primary wound. While they fear abandonment, they may also test it with a vengeance. If they can get mom to reject them, it validates their primal fear of being defective, and that they will be rejected and abandoned.

We must enter our adoptive relationships with an ability to separate our worth from our role—this is imperative. We can't fix our child, and our child certainly can't fix us or our marriage! If we're infertile before we adopt, we will probably be infertile after we adopt. We can, however, educate ourselves, seek outside intervention from an attachment or other specialist, make sure we've managed our issues well, and determine to provide a safe environment for that child's heart to heal.

There are no guarantees, but this is a good start. If you've adopted as a couple, dads must appreciate mom's vulnerable position, and support her. Single moms might cultivate knowledgeable, empathetic support systems who understand this dynamic, or are willing to learn. Wherever we are in this process, hope and healing await.

DAILY SESSIONS: WEEK FOUR

Here's what I want you to do. Find a quiet, secluded place so you won't be tempted to role-play before God. Just be there as simply and honestly as you can manage. The focus will shift from you to God, and you will begin to sense his grace.
—Matthew 6:6 MSG

SOME THOUGHTS BEFORE YOU BEGIN:

- Offer yourself to the Lord each day . . . just the way you are!

- Set aside time to think about and record your answers to each day's questions.

- Ask God to quiet your heart and mind; invite Him into your process. He is the only one who truly knows you, your child, your family, and your story.

- Notice and make note of your feelings. Give yourself permission to feel the wide range of emotions certain to surface.

- Be honest . . . no over-spiritualizing, criticism, or judgment allowed.

- Give God permission to love you!

- There is no right or wrong answer. Dispense with "shoulds."

DAY ONE:

Detours

In his heart a man plans his course, but the LORD determines his steps.
—Proverbs 16:9

*for he guards the course of the just and protects
the way of his faithful ones.*
—Proverbs 2:8

BEFORE YOU BEGIN:

- Pray. Ask God to quiet your mind and help you listen to His voice.
- Determine to be gut-level honest in your responses.
- Commit yourself to the Lord's healing process for you.

QUESTIONS:

1. Write one sentence accurately describing the place you didn't belong.

2. What was your plan to become a parent?

3. How has God guarded and protected you on this journey?

4. Though you may not have chosen to be in the place you didn't belong, how has God used this in your life?

NOTICING:

What physical reactions and feelings did you notice?

PRAYER:

Thank You, Father, that my journey has not surprised You. You have guarded and protected me every step of the way. Help me see Your purpose and Your redeeming love.

DAY TWO:

Once Upon A Time

And the LORD said to Moses, "I will do the very thing you have asked,
because I am pleased with you and I know you by name."
—Exodus 33:17

May the God of hope fill you with all joy and peace as
you trust in him, so that you may overflow with hope by
the power of the Holy Spirit.
—Romans 15:13

BEFORE YOU BEGIN:

- Pray. Ask God to quiet your mind and help you listen to His voice.
- Determine to be gut-level honest in your responses.
- Commit yourself to the Lord's healing process for you.

QUESTIONS:

1. In previous chapters, we identified our adoption expectations and realities, explored our child's compromised beginning, and named the place we didn't belong. In Chapter Three, Day Three, we considered the losses our collisions created. Before we move on to Part Two, let's take some time to consider the sum total of our adoption experience to this point in time. Write your story here. Don't forget to include your expectations, realities, and collision (use additional paper if you need more room).

2. Read your story out loud to Jesus. Check here when you have done this _____.

3. Prayerfully take your story to the foot of the cross. Entrust it to Jesus.
   (1 Peter 5:7, Matthew 11:28, Philippians 4:6, 2 Corinthians 4:8, Exodus 33:14)

Now, rest again. Listen for His voice. What do you hear? What does He say?

NOTICING:

What physical reactions and feelings did you notice?

PRAYER:

Oh Father, I place my hope in You alone. I'm beginning to realize the place I didn't think I belonged is Your starting place. I pray for the courage to continue.

DAY THREE:

Grieve Our Past Losses

. . . Hannah replied, "I am a woman who is deeply troubled. I have not been drinking wine or beer; I was pouring out my soul to the LORD. Do not take your servant for a wicked woman; I have been praying here out of my great anguish and grief."
—1 Samuel 1:15-16

"Adoption loss is the only trauma in the world whose victims are expected by the whole of society to be grateful."
—Unknown

BEFORE YOU BEGIN:

- Pray. Ask God to quiet your mind and help you listen to His voice.
- Determine to be gut-level honest in your responses.
- Commit yourself to the Lord's healing process for you.

Our futures look and feel different from what we planned for our lives. While this brings new opportunities for blessing and helping others, it usually means we've lost some things along the way. We will have difficulty fully embracing our permanent-alternate-route until first saying good-bye to our dreams in the rearview mirror. This work won't be done in a day, or even a week. Healing generally takes six to eighteen months. We may need to revisit this from time to time, or seek professional help. That's OK. But, it's important to acknowledge these astronomical changes, and manage them in healthy, life-giving ways. When we dig deep, most of the burdens we carry grow from our losses.

The Backpack: "Today I simply sat before the Lord and began to unpack those burdens I feel lying heavy on my heart. I imagined a backpack, filled with stones, weighing me down. One by one I removed a stone, held it carefully in my hand, named it, and set it down at the feet of Jesus. I entrusted each of those named stones to His care, knowing I could only truly deal with one at a time. Collectively, they paralyzed me. I find myself struggling to free myself from the load, or just succumbing." *(Journal entry, anonymous mom, October 10, 2010.)*

QUESTIONS:

1. Take your "backpack" with you to that quiet, secluded place. Ask God to help you name the stones weighing you down. Start your list here. For those who prefer a more concrete exercise, find an old backpack or fanny-pack. Add rocks or stones. Grab a permanent marker to name your stones, and then carry your load to a quiet place to unpack.

2. One by one, lay them at Jesus' feet. Check here when you have completed this _____.

Grief work is vitally important for our healing, and for our ability to help our adopted children do their grief work (part of mitigating the damage of their five-story-fall). In her book *Attaching in Adoption: Practical Tools for Today's Parents,* Deborah Gray explains, "When parents have not worked through their own grief, it is much more difficult for them to accompany children into grief work. Rather than having the strength to support children in grief, they find their own unresolved grief facing them."

Grief wears many masks, such as sadness, anger, or aggressive behavior. Our American culture allows little time or space for grief, or for diversity in its expression. Family and friends seldom acknowledge the "invisible" grief we carry. For single parents, the loss or absence of a life partner to help carry this new challenge may resurface. Therefore, it becomes imperative we acknowledge our losses, carve out time in our schedule to manage this process, and simply begin. We can't be free from grief until we've walked through it.

The Grief Process:

Following are six classic stages of grief for adults:

1. Shock and surprise ("No! I can't believe this!")

2. Denial

3. Anger

4. Bargaining (with God, or others, to arrange a different outcome)

5. Sadness or mourning

6. Resolution (we learn to manage the loss and go on in life)

In real life, these steps are seldom linear. Sometimes, our grieving process requires revisiting steps. Unrealistic expectations of grief can also be a setback to healing. Grief is messy, and often more closely resembles a winding road than a straight one. However, it remains an important journey if healing is our goal.

3. Review your "backpack" list from the previous page. Identify which stage of grief you believe is relative to each stone. Put the corresponding number (from the stages of grief listed above) next to each named stone. Check here when you have completed this _____.

4. Write a prayer to God. Share your grief with Him. Listen for what He wants to tell you.

NOTICING:

What physical reactions and feelings did you notice?

PRAYER:

Father, thank You for understanding my grief and having all the time in the world to help me deal with this. Please walk with me on this journey. I need Your peace and rest.

DAY FOUR:

Embrace Our New Reality

The Spirit of the Sovereign LORD is on me, because the LORD has anointed me to preach good news to the poor. He has sent me to bind up the brokenhearted, to proclaim freedom for the captives and release for the prisoners, to proclaim the year of the LORD's favor and the day of vengeance of our God, to comfort all who mourn, and provide for those who grieve in Zion—to bestow on them a crown of beauty instead of ashes, the oil of gladness instead of mourning, and a garment of praise instead of a spirit of despair.
—Isaiah 61:1-3

Then a great and powerful wind tore the mountains apart and shattered the rocks before the LORD, but the LORD was not in the wind. After the wind there was an earthquake, but the LORD was not in the earthquake. After the earthquake came a fire, but the LORD was not in the fire. And after the fire came a gentle whisper.
—1 Kings 19:11-12

BEFORE YOU BEGIN:

- Pray. Ask God to quiet your mind and help you listen to His voice.
- Determine to be gut-level honest in your responses.
- Commit yourself to the Lord's healing process for you.

The metaphorical whirlwinds, earthquakes, and trials by fire our children thrust into our homes threaten to consume us. Our new realities may carry enormous pain, maybe regret. This daily exercise is not meant to minimize those experiences with pat answers or clichés, but to point you to Jesus and His truth and grace. Our new realities do include shattered dreams, collisions, and detours. Suffering, however, does have a sweet side! The Lord longs to bind up our broken hearts, free us from the prisons we create, comfort and provide for us when we grieve, bestow on us a crown of beauty, and fill us with gladness and praise. This is the truth of our new reality, the piece we can embrace!

QUESTIONS:

1. What is your response to His invitation in Isaiah 61:1-3? Tell God your response in the space below. Ask Him for what you need to make this real in your life.

2. In the midst of our chaos, God's voice often comes as a whisper. Right now, envision Jesus at your side, smiling at you. As He draws close, He cups His hands over your ear to whisper a secret just for you . . . what is He saying?

NOTICING:

What physical reactions and feelings did you notice?

PRAYER:

Father, I trust You to help me grieve my losses so I can embrace the future You have for me, regardless of the needs of my child. Help me listen for Your whisper. I'm ready for the journey back into Your arms.

CONCLUSION OF PART ONE

My Dear Friend,

We're Homeward Bound! Thank you for hanging in there! We've covered some tough and painful territory these past weeks, not unlike cleaning out a nasty wound before healing can occur. Cleansing paves the way for a speedy recovery. Your work hasn't been wasted. No more band-aids over the gaping wounds of our hearts!

As we journey on, I pray God's spirit will continue to LEAD you toward the healing you seek and desperately want as we:

Leave the past at the foot of the cross.

Exchange our lies for His truth.

Allow Him access to our hearts and embrace His plan.

Determine to finish the race He has called us to, with a renewed sense of His grace.

His touch is personal, His love unfathomable, and His truth unalterable. I pray these truths become more real in tangible ways in the weeks ahead. We're going to leave isolation, fear, and depression in the dust, and allow God to lead us back into His arms!

One way we'll do that is through the acquisition and use of some new tools. Each of us has a toolbox filled with coping strategies, life lessons, scriptural truths, and more. Some of us regularly tidy up our boxes, others manage with disheveled ones. Whatever their state, we're going to dust 'em off, examine what's inside, get rid of ineffective tools, and add new tools in the weeks ahead.

If you're completing this study as part of a healing support group, I pray your relationships in the group deepen as you build a safe and trusting support community. Please, continue making time for you. We may have taken detours, but there are no shortcuts to healing!

Now . . . on to Part Two!

With Great Affection on Our Shared Journey,
Paula

WEEKLY SUMMARY AND MEETING

Insights, Thoughts, Comments, and Questions from Reading and Daily Exercises:

How God met me this week:

Support Group Meeting Notes:

PART TWO:
Right Into His Arms

WEEK FIVE:
Homeward Bound
Wounds, Self-Care, and Forgiveness

To the Jews who had believed him, Jesus said, "If you hold to my teaching, you are really my disciples. Then you will know the truth, and the truth will set you free."
—John 8:31-32

Therefore, as God's chosen people, holy and dearly loved, clothe your-selves with compassion, kindness, humility, gentleness and patience. Bear with each other and forgive whatever grievances you may have against one another. Forgive as the Lord forgave you.
—Colossians 3:12-13

Over the past weeks, we've examined our expectations and adoption realities, identi-fied our children's compromised beginnings, and discovered how those collided with our personal wounds to deliver us to a place we didn't belong. Efforts to regain control of our lives exhaust us. While we may not be able to change many of our circumstances, we can add new tools to our toolbox to increase the likelihood we'll arrive safely at the destination for which our hearts are created. We're homeward bound!

Tracy's Story

Tracy inched her way down the plane's slender aisle, stowed her baggage, and slid into her assigned seat. She couldn't remember the last time she'd gotten away without her daughter. As a single mom, finding help with her teenage daughter was difficult. She hoped this weekend away to visit college roommates would help pull her from her perpetual funk. Tracy settled into her seat, opened a new book, and tried to ignore the flight attendant's safety speech booming overhead.

"*. . . and please secure your own mask before assisting others.*"

Stunned, Tracy dropped her book to brush away tears threatening to spill from her eyes. Thoughts and feelings she fought to keep at bay engulfed her. No wonder she felt overwhelmed! She spent her days outfitting others with their masks, while she gasped for air!

"That was my 'aha' moment," Tracy explained. "I did spend that weekend with friends, and it was great. But, I realized I needed professional help. I felt pretty scared about what was happening inside me. My world kept getting smaller and darker. I felt exhausted. Nobody tried harder at this thing than I did, but my life continued to unravel around me. When I returned home, I called a friend who worked at my church, and asked if she could recommend a good counselor for me. I was in so much pain, ready to do anything to get out from under the suffocating anguish and guilt I felt. Somehow, I knew God was using this pain to get my attention; it worked!"

Tracy called the counselor and made an appointment. More importantly, she determined to engage in the counseling process. "I knew Cassie was a tool God provided to help me," she said. "I finally admitted I needed help, that there was no magic wand or quick fix for what I was dealing with." Empowered by the knowledge, insights, and tools she gained over the weeks, Tracy embraced this hard work; she believed God led her here, and she would be successful.

"I remember the first time I met with Cassie," Tracy said. "I shared that I felt overwhelmed and sad due to years of compounded disappointments related to my adoptions. Cassie asked what thoughts, feelings, and behaviors went with that," Tracy continued. "After thinking a moment, I told her my thoughts were conflicted, but I knew I didn't want to live like this anymore. I felt exhausted, sad, angry, and fearful; I constantly multitasked and pushed myself. Cassie was wonderful. She listened, asked good questions, and never told me I 'should' do or not do anything. Anyway, that afternoon she sent me home with a tool, like a questionnaire. I answered the questions as honestly as I could before we met again to review my answers. Neither of us was surprised at the outcome. I clearly struggled with depression. That was a relief, and a turning point for me."

Tracy met regularly with Cassie, spent time in God's word, and began identifying and working through the issues contributing to her depression. The most significant knowledge Tracy gained, however, was learning about her core wounds, the lies she believed, and the false identity she had created to deal with them. "I was afraid of failure and rejection; this stemmed from my childhood. I believed the lie that if I failed, I would be rejected. Like all kids, I created ways to deal with my fears. I didn't even know I was doing it, they were just childish defenses: my 'little-girl tools,' as Cassie called them. I became all about production, striving, keeping busy, and accomplishing things. Throughout the years, this need to accomplish and produce (and not get rejected) got tangled up with my sense of worth as a person. All my multitasking was really me doubling my efforts to be a good mom, to keep from failing so I wouldn't be rejected by my daughter. I now realize all those things contributed to my collision. Without understanding my daughter's fundamental need to protect her heart by rejecting me as a mother, I immediately personalized it because of *my* wounds. That striving/rejection thing has continued in our relationship for years! Cassie helped me see I needed some new tools. My little-girl tools weren't working anymore. Cassie taught me how to prayerfully take off the old lies and ask God to replace them with His truth. With time and practice, the truth did begin to set me free!"

Tracy also learned to separate her worth as a person from her role as a mother. While she longs for a mutually-satisfying relationship with her daughter, she knows it might not happen because of her daughter's compromised beginnings. "I still pray for her, want the best for her, and believe God will continue drawing my daughter to Himself. But, I no longer beat myself up over her poor choices. I know I'm a good enough mom to this child God entrusted to me."

—*Tracy, single adoptive mother of a school-aged girl from foster care.*

Kate's Story

Kate and Jason thrived in their role as parents of three active boys. They also understood countless children around the world needed families, and they wanted to help. Their growing desire to adopt led them to Africa. With help from a reputable agency, they adopted an infant son; two years later Alissa, their toddler-aged daughter, joined the family from the same country.

"Although I had read books and attended adoption training, Alissa's reactive attachment behaviors still knocked the wind out of me," Kate said. "For the first couple of months after she came home, she acted just like our son had. She wanted me to hold her all the time. I remember the exact moment she made her first statement that the last thing she wanted was to belong to me. We were at the grocery store when she reached for a stranger to hold her. Somewhat bewildered, he took her in his arms. When I reached to take her back, she clung to this man and began to cry. Things only got worse from there. In the days ahead, Alissa screamed incessantly. She also bit, hit, and kicked me. I knew she was trying to protect her heart from the unendurable nightmare of losing another mother, but those were very painful months. Over the next couple of years, Jason and I did the best we could to convince her heart we weren't leaving, and, slowly, I think she's starting to believe it."

A few years later, Kate's job took her to Alissa's birth country. Inquisitive by nature, she sought answers to the growing list of her daughter's disabilities. While visiting the orphanage from which Alissa came, Kate enjoyed a precious visit with Kate's former caregiver. At last, she could ask the questions plaguing her about Alissa's birth. "I knew Alissa was born because of an attempted abortion," Kate said. "But I didn't know the details. Somehow, over time, I managed to romanticize it, attributing the most altruistic motives to her birth mother. Maybe that's why the truth was so shocking to me."

Alissa's mother took chemicals to abort her, then went to the hospital to deliver the dead fetus. Instead of emerging lifeless from her mother's body, Alissa cried. Shocked the baby was still alive, her birth mother tried to choke her to death before nurses whisked her away. Alissa arrived at the orphanage the following day, a mere three pounds, but alive.

"I wasn't sure how I would make it through the day," Kate said after learning the details of her daughter's traumatic birth. "I didn't tell a soul. That night I lay awake for the longest time, wrestling with this horrible secret, but I couldn't cry."

Kate had planned to meet with the birth mother the next day. She wondered how in the world she would endure that meeting! "God gave me the strength, and I'm glad I met with her," she said. "I felt wonder, mystery, and frustration as we talked for a couple of hours. She was strikingly beautiful. At a turn of the face, or an angle of the eyes, I felt I was looking right at Alissa. I was very disappointed, because she just wouldn't engage in questions about herself. Now I realize the frustration I felt was really an underlying rage—she tried to kill my daughter twice: the least she could do was tell me something about herself for me to tell Alissa someday!"

Alissa now lives with organic brain damage which manifests itself in the areas of speech, fine motor skill difficulties, and executive brain function problems. Kate and Jason strive to find interventions to maximize her potential and mitigate her five-story fall. When the dust settles and evening quiet blankets their household, the greater task remains for Kate and Jason . . . how to forgive the birth mother who willfully damaged their child.

Kate understands forgiveness is a process, not a once-and-for-all deal. She allowed herself to acknowledge her hurt and anger. As the guardian of Alissa's story, she prayerfully selected a small group of trusted friends with whom to talk. Although Kate anguished over the details of her child's history, she understood she needed to forgive Alissa's birth mother simply because Christ forgave her. After several months, Kate chose to forgive, and began putting this hurt behind her. Anger raises its ugly head from time to time, reminding Kate she's only human. She continues to choose forgiveness, and asks God to make her patient with the process. Alissa will always live within the bondage of her brain damage; forgiveness prevented this tragedy from claiming more casualties.

—*Kate and Jason, adoptive parents of two children from Africa.*

WOUNDS

In the process of trying to protect our hearts, we can become crippled, compensating, afraid to embrace the wounds separating us from what our hearts cry out for—healing, restoration, and belonging.

Healing requires identifying and tending to our wounds. We have all sinned, and we have all been sinned against; humans are wounded. Additionally, our socialization as American Christian women most likely means we've been taught to deny ourselves to the point of extinction. However, we can't love our brother (or children, husband, etc.) as ourselves until we learn to love God first, then ourselves.

Identify and Tend to Your Wounds

We sustain wounds early, and often, in life. Wounds range from misunderstandings to outrageous wrongs done to us. How we think about a hurtful event affects our feelings and behavior. Wounds provide fertile soil for lies to take root, grow, and consume us. In defending ourselves we create a false identity, based on more lies, to deal with the increasing pain.

Let me explain. One afternoon, when I was about five years old, my dad was pushing me on a swing in our backyard. I fell off and got hurt. Not badly, but I could have used a hug. Instead, he told me to brush it off and get back on the swing. We were having fun. I loved being with my dad. He didn't intend to hurt me by pushing me too hard, or using harsh words. This event, over the course of a lifetime, is hardly noteworthy. However, I began to believe a lie that afternoon: when hurt, I should minimize it and move on. I believed this would protect me from my father's rejection I feared would come if I cried and carried on. The false identity I created over many years was tough, unflappable, and able to deal with anything. The purpose of my external identity was avoiding rejection.

The constant rejection I felt from one adopted daughter assaulted my false identity. Can you see the collision coming here? I finally had to identify and admit the "little-girl tool" I created at five years of age was inadequate for adult challenges. Minimizing and moving on wasn't working for me anymore.

We construct false identities over a lifetime, based on lies we believe. Not dealing with the lies keeps healing at bay, and holds us in bondage. When we acknowledge and identify our wounds, we can exchange the lies we believed for God's truth. In prayer, we take off the old and put on the new. Metaphorically, we become naked before God. He wants to clothe us with His truth, thereby replacing lies and false identities. This great exchange allows us to shed our false identity, discover who God created us to be, then walk in freedom.

Several years ago, I drove through beautiful mountains to our satellite office on Colorado's Western Slope. As I drove, I prayed, "God, would you please show me the truth You want to clothe me with?" The bold barrenness of the aspen trees that fall day struck me. They looked naked. As I pondered their nakedness, an analogy emerged. God began answering my prayer. Just as the wind and elements had blown away the trees' dead leaves, exposing the underlying barrenness, so had the storms of life blown away the deadness of lies I had believed. The trees' barren state was not shameful; it is a natural part of their life cycle. The roots remain firmly planted, allowing nutrients and water from the soil to sustain them. New growth will appear to replace fallen leaves in the right season, with God causing the growth. The trees could do nothing to rush the naked season. As I learned to listen to the Lord's voice, I started hearing truths like: My grace is sufficient, the fullness of Christ dwells in you, you can do all things through Christ who strengthens you, I see you as wholly righteous because of the blood of Jesus,

I am your Father, and you are My beloved daughter. Buds of new growth began to appear.

Wounds are normal. We have all created little-girl tools to help manage them. However, at some point in our lives, if we're honest, we admit they no longer work. Single-handedly, our children with challenges dismantle and expose the lies and gaping wounds we tried ferociously to protect! Taking time to identify and examine our little-girl tools in light of God's truth provides an opportunity to consider grievous events from God's perspective, and choose the great exchange. When we "take off the old" and "put on the new," we take a giant step toward personal healing, which is experiencing the reality of our identity in Christ.

SELF-CARE

For most of us, self-care plummeted to the bottom of our to-do list ages ago. Our commitment to heal requires putting it back on our radar and into our schedules. Learning to nourish ourselves provides deposits to our emotional bank accounts. We've all learned the hard way that, if the only activity our account sees is withdrawals, we'll eventually go bankrupt. How long will our reserves hold out? The answer varies from woman to woman. However, unless deposits to our account equal or exceed withdrawals, the outcome is guaranteed for all of us!

So, where do we get "emotional income"? Anything nourishing to our body, mind, or soul pays us emotionally. This can be physical exercise, reading a good book, or visually savoring the beauty of art or a brilliant sunrise. Worship, music, or coffee and conversation with a dear friend all contribute to our well-being and bolster our accounts.

Take time to consider your dreams. What do you crave? In learning to care for ourselves, there are many right answers. Let the following suggestions prime your creative pump. Jot down an idea or two of what you think would nourish you in the margin. Make a priority of including something from each of the following categories in your schedule.

Mental: Our mental health and well-being may be missing in action. We know from Scripture the importance God places on renewing our minds. Self-care might include daily Scripture reading and memorizing meaningful verses. Perhaps you could benefit from counseling or mental health services. Time to read a good book, engage in adult conversation, or take an online course might be the nourishment you crave. Whatever it is, start somewhere as soon as you can.

Physical: Take care of yourself. If you don't, no one else will.

- Eat a balanced diet.
- Rest, get enough sleep for you.
- Rest, take a day of rest each week (God did!).
- Rest, learn to enter the "Sabbath rest" of God, in the midst of your circumstances.
- Exercise—it doesn't have to be a work out, just move more.
- Laugh.
- Change your hairstyle.
- Get a facial.
- Enjoy a massage.
- Lose weight.
- Eat chocolate!
- Take a hot bubble bath, with a do not disturb sign on the door.
- Buy a new shade of lipstick.
- Get a manicure . . . or give yourself one!

Social: Children with challenges can cause social relationships to fall by the wayside. Friends may not invite us over anymore because of our child's behavior. And what about old friends, church community, and family members who don't understand, and become constant withdrawals from our emotional bank account? We are still created for community. Maybe it's time to begin developing new relationships (more on that in Week Seven). Start small. Call a friend or someone new you'd like to be friends with. Go for coffee. Accept help from others. Resist isolation, and find ways to make social interaction deposits to your emotional bank account.

Spiritual: We are spiritual beings, created for fellowship with God. If you have pulled away from God as a result of your adoption experience, this might be a good time to reconsider your beliefs about Him. Ask God to replace any false beliefs with His truth. He promises to stick closer than a brother (Prov 18:24), to comfort and rescue us (numerous verses in Psalms), and give us rest from our burdens (Matt 11:18). We are the apple of His eye. God delights in us. Nothing we can do could make Him love us more.

FORGIVENESS

Now we're getting down to some nitty-gritty stuff. While I believe a spirit of forgiveness should mark the life of every Christian, practicing forgiveness is more problematic. Scripture seems pretty clear on this one. If God forgives me, I have no basis to withhold forgiveness from others.

As moms of children with challenges, we're faced with lots of things gone wrong. Birth families injured our children, we behaved badly at times, husbands checked out, friends and family members failed us, adoption social workers and agencies misled us, and the list goes on. The weight of un-forgiveness sucks the spiritual life from us, creating unwalled prisons more secure than Fort Knox.

Getting a grip on forgiveness accelerates our healing. Dr. Steve Stephens and Alice Gray present learning to forgive as a process, not a once-and-for-all activity, in their book, *The Worn Out Woman*. They note, " . . . the failure to deal with hurts is one of the primary reasons women feel exhausted and weary. Carrying a load of resentment or guilt takes a terrible toll—physically, emotionally, and spiritually." They say learning to forgive is a process we move through when we:

1. Admit our hurt and anger.
2. Talk it out.
3. Remember why forgiveness is necessary.
4. Choose forgiveness.
5. Put the hurt behind you.
6. Be patient with the process.
7. Forgive yourself.

Forgiveness is a key to unlock the door of our personal prison. When we give the gift of forgiveness, it comes back to bless us with peace and rest.

Before We Continue

As we move into this week's daily exercises, please feel free to go at your own pace. Be gentle with yourself. This is a guided journey, but there is no predetermined destination. Take the time you need. Continue asking God to guide and direct your healing process. You may realize you could benefit from professional counseling. That's great! If you're participating in a healing support group, be sure to talk with your leader about this, and ask for a referral to an adoption-savvy counselor or mental health professional. The following exercises are tools for you; use them as needed.

DAILY SESSIONS: WEEK FIVE

Fear not, for I have redeemed you;
I have called you by name; you are mine.
—Isaiah 43:1b

SOME THOUGHTS BEFORE YOU BEGIN:

- Offer yourself to the Lord each day . . . just the way you are!

- Set aside time to think about and record your answers to each day's questions.

- Ask God to quiet your heart and mind; invite Him into your process. He is the only one who truly knows you, your child, your family, and your story.

- Notice and make note of your feelings. Give yourself permission to feel the wide range of emotions certain to surface.

- Be honest . . . no over-spiritualizing, criticism, or judgment allowed.

- Give God permission to love you!

- There is no right or wrong answer. Dispense with "shoulds."

This week we'll dust off our toolboxes, examine what's inside, get rid of ineffective tools, and put in some new ones. We'll add:

- Listening Prayer
- Thought-Feeling Diagram
- Emotion-Resolution Process
- Emotional-Assessment Tool
- Forgiveness

DAY ONE:

Understanding Our Core Wounds

*Do not lie to each other, since you have taken off your old self with
its practices and have put on the new self, which is being renewed in
knowledge in the image of its Creator.*
—Colossians 3:9-10

BEFORE YOU BEGIN:

- Pray. Ask God to quiet your mind and help you listen to His voice.
- Determine to be gut-level honest in your responses.
- Commit yourself to the Lord's healing process for you.

QUESTIONS:

Healing is a process. If we want the benefits, we must do our part—time and hard
work. But the real price we pay is ignoring God's invitation to enter into His redemptive work in our lives. As we ask God's spirit to expose lies we created to deal with our
wounds, and learn to replace them with God's truth, His transforming power changes
us from the inside out. Tracy saw God begin His transforming work in her through
listening prayer.

Listening Prayer: Determined to discover the root of her depression, Tracy eager-
ly applied new tools Cassie taught her during counseling. One of these was listening
prayer. Although Cassie initially guided Tracy through the process, Tracy soon learned
that listening prayer was simply a way of listening for God's response to her prayerful
requests for insight and healing. She believed God knew her inside and out, He knew
the source of her wounds and the little-girl tools she had created to deal with them.
Since those tools didn't work anymore, she felt ready to listen. Tracy set aside time in a
quiet place to meet with God (not the laundry room or kitchen!). She bowed her head,
committed the time to the Lord, and asked the Holy Spirit to guide her process.

Tracy immediately thought about her daughter. Cassie had taught her to identify the
feelings behind her thoughts. She recognized that when she thought of her daughter

she felt regret. Tracy wondered before the Lord what she regretted. Additional thoughts came to her . . . she regretted not getting help sooner, and now it felt too late. Tracy continued thinking about this regret, and asked God to show her what was behind it. Tracy waited, then whispered to herself, "Guilt . . . I should have done more to help her. I feel responsible and sad." Tears trickled down her cheeks; her stomach burned. Thanks to her experience with Cassie and listening prayer, she knew she was getting close to the source of her wound. Tracy asked God to show her what was behind her "shoulds." The answer flowed into her conscious thoughts before she finished the question, "I'm tired and resentful of the shoulds," Tracy thought. "I've lived a lifetime of them, all over, everywhere. My wound is about needing approval . . . and not being rejected!"

Once Tracy identified her fear of rejection, she recognized the lies she had constructed to overcome her sense of inadequacy were what drove her to accomplish and produce; "should" fueled her behavior. She asked God to reveal His truth about her fear of rejection. Tracy began to sense God's personal love and unconditional acceptance of her.

Tracy's core wound:	*fear of rejection.*
Little-girl tools:	*"should" . . . and fill in the blank. Work, activity, production, achievement, multitasking, etc. (Can you see how that led to feeling exhausted and overwhelmed?)*
God's truth:	*You are the apple of My eye. You are a new creation.*

1. How would Tracy's core wound contribute to her adoption collision?

2. **Learning to Listen:** God is gentle and compassionate. He will guide your journey as you are ready and as you trust Him. He will never leave you or forsake you. The purpose is freedom and healing. Those who are in Christ Jesus are not condemned. Quiet your mind before Him, pray, and invite the Holy Spirit to guide your thoughts, then ask God to show you where He wants to begin. Identify your feelings and write them here:

_____   _____   _____   _____

Continue asking God what lies behind your thoughts and feelings. This may proceed as "layers" or "steps" leading you toward the wound, the lie you believed, and the discovery of what little-girl tools you used to create your false identity. Ask God to reveal a wound and the lie you have believed. Listen for His answer. Write it down. Keep listening as you ask God to show you the tools you constructed. Keep going, we're almost there! Ask God to reveal His truth to you.

My wound: _____

The lie I believed: _____

My little-girl tools: _____

God's truth: _____

3. **Application:** The Great Exchange! *Take off the old and put on the new* (Ephesians 4:22-24). Make this application intentional and prayerful. Write a prayer to God. Tell Him you want to take off the lie (name it!), and put on His truth (name it!). Tell Him you choose to take Him at His word.

NOTICING:

What physical reactions and feelings did you notice?

PRAYER:

Father, thank You for understanding everything about my core wounds and the lies I've believed. Bring these into Your light through Your Holy Spirit, so I can surrender them to Your control and be free. Help me exchange them for Your truth. I'm so glad You love and accept me just as I am!

DAY TWO:

Feeling, Nothing More Than Feeling . . . (Or is it?)

*Do not conform any longer to the pattern of this world, but be trans-
formed by the renewing of your mind. Then you will be able to test
and approve what God's will is—his good, pleasing, and perfect will.*
—Romans 12:2

*Finally brothers, whatever is true, whatever is noble, whatever is right,
whatever is pure, whatever is lovely, whatever is admirable—if anything is excellent or praiseworthy—think about such things. Whatever
you have learned or received or heard from me, or seen in me—put it
into practice. And the God of peace will be with you.*
—Philippians 4:8-9

BEFORE YOU BEGIN:

- Pray. Ask God to quiet your mind and help you listen to His voice.
- Determine to be gut-level honest in your responses.
- Commit yourself to the Lord's healing process for you.

QUESTIONS:

1. The diagram below illustrates one way to understand the mental, emotional, and behavioral process many of us go through when we respond to events in our lives. Recent brain research indicates some people may need a more experiential, whole-brain way to access and process these connections. Use the following diagram, explanation, and exercise as a tool if it fits and makes sense for how you're wired.

Our thoughts about an event influence our feelings, which in turn affect our behavior. Learning to "reframe" an event in our thoughts can change our feelings and subsequent behavior. What we do with our feelings about the event, not the event itself, generally determines our behavior. If we want to change an emotional or behavioral outcome, one place to intervene is at the thought level (Romans 8:6).

Rachel Harrison, LCPC, NCC, therapist, and adoptive mother of children with challenges states: "Approximately 10 percent of our thoughts are in our conscious awareness. Now, if we are working to capture our thoughts in order to shift our feelings and behavior, we can only do that with the 10 percent we are aware of. The goal of most counseling is to make the subconscious conscious, so that people can choose and shift their thoughts, feelings, and behaviors."

Listening prayer provides one way God can bring our subconscious and/or His thoughts into our conscious, providing us with the opportunity to intentionally exchange lies for truth.

Think back to Tracy, and how she processed her daughter's rejection. Keep in mind anger can be one face of sadness. Scenario One depicts Tracy's likely response.

Scenario One: After being caught in a lie, Tracy's daughter raged, screaming she hated Tracy, she wanted to hurt her, and she wished she had never been adopted! Shocked by her daughter's remarks, Tracy thinks she is a bad mom for raising a child who is so disrespectful. She feels like a failure, and fears continued rejection. Tracy withdraws from her daughter, and pours her energy into work and church activities, determined not to fail in other areas of her life.

Now read Scenario Two, which reframes Tracy's thoughts about her daughter's behavior.

Scenario Two: After being caught in a lie, Tracy's daughter raged, screaming she hated Tracy, she wanted to hurt her, and she wished she had never been adopted! Tracy realized her daughter's response was an attempt to maintain control of the relationship, and not submit to her authority. She felt compassion for her daughter, knowing she really needed and wanted a mom. She calmly affirmed her love for her daughter, and allowed her an opportunity to redo her behavior. Both Tracy and her daughter then resumed normal family activities.

1. Which scenario is healthier for Tracy and her daughter? Why?

2. Think of one or two key events in your adoption experience which caused you grief or anxiety, and resulted in you behaving in a way you'd like to change. Write your experience below:

Now, reframe the event by changing your thought, feeling, behavior sequence. Write it below:

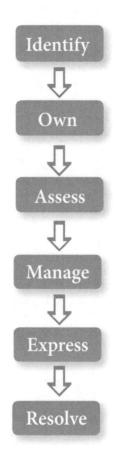

3. The above diagram illustrates a process to help us effectively manage our emotions. Don't make it hard. This is just a tool to help us slow down and think before we react. When you find yourself in an emotionally-charged situation, take a deep breath, and mentally walk yourself through this process. Identify your feeling, and then own it. Nobody can "make" you mad without your permission. Do a quick assessment. Would a typical person in this situation have a similar response? Manage it. This means you control your emotions, determine exactly how you want to respond, and then express yourself. This may be stating something like, "I feel sad when I see you make this kind of poor choice."

What do you think happens if the first thing we do with our emotions is to express them? Why do you think it might be important to identify, own, assess, and manage our emotions before we express them? How does this relate to your current adoption reality?

4. **Emotional Assessment:** The following emotional scale provides a simple tool to assess (Step Three above) our emotional response to events in our lives. For example, if we rate our response to a situation or comment an eight, but most people would consider it a three, we know that situation or comment hit a wound. Ouch! This quick tool helps us assess our emotions and manage them before we express the emotion. This tool is also an effective indicator of unresolved or poorly managed issues. When we over-respond, we can ask God to reveal our wound, what lies we have believed, and replace them with His truth. This helps to bring the unconscious into the conscious, and provides an opportunity to exchange the lie for God's truth. Caution: Our personal pain sometimes blinds our objectivity. We may fuel our wounds and reinforce old paradigms through our self-talk, or by the people we choose to talk with about our situations. While these folks are often well-meaning, they sometimes work against our ability to compassionately reframe such experiences. Think of a situation where you know you clearly over-responded. Think through the situation based on this assessment model and what we've just learned about the cause of our wounds. Write it below:

1   2   3   4   5   6   7   8   9   10

5. Our adoptions have provided numerous opportunities to over-react, express our emotions before managing them, or respond in anger to the loss and sadness we've experienced. This may have led to regret, fractured relationships, or disappointment with ourselves and others. Write an apology letter—or letters—in the space below (even if it's to yourself!):

NOTICING:

What physical reactions and feelings did you notice?

PRAYER:

Oh Father, thank You for creating our emotions. Help me to manage mine and use them for Your glory.

DAY THREE:

Self-Care

*"Why do you ask me about what is good?" Jesus replied. "There is only
One who is good. If you want to enter life, obey the commandments."
"Which ones?" the man inquired.
Jesus replied, "'Do not murder, do not commit adultery, do not steal,
do not give false testimony, honor your father and mother,' and 'love
your neighbor as yourself.'"*
—Matthew 19:17-19

BEFORE YOU BEGIN:

- Pray. Ask God to quiet your mind and help you listen to His voice.
- Determine to be gut-level honest in your responses.
- Commit yourself to the Lord's healing process for you.

QUESTIONS:

1. Let's take a quick inventory of our emotional bank accounts. In the table below,
   list all your nourishing relationships and activities in the "deposit" column. Now,
   identify and write down those relationships, activities, responsibilities, etc. that
   extract withdrawals from your emotional bank account.

DEPOSIT	WITHDRAWAL

2. What changes do you want to make?

3. List five major activities you did this week. How much time did you spend on each? Where could you find one hour to do something just for you?

    a.

    b.

    c.

    d.

    e.

4. Complete the table on the following page by listing ten things you enjoy doing. Jot down the last time you remember doing each one, then schedule time (even if it's way out in the future) to do this again. Just putting it down and planning empowers us.

5. "Many of us have made a virtue out of deprivation . . . we strive to be good, to be nice, to be helpful, to be unselfish. We want to be generous, of service, of the world. But what we really want is to be left alone . . . afraid to appear selfish, we lose our self. We become self-destructive."
   —Julia Cameron, *The Artist's Way*

In what ways have you allowed your adoption journey to become self-destructive?

THINGS I ENJOY DOING	THE LAST TIME I DID THIS	WHEN I WILL DO IT!

NOTICING:

What physical reactions and feelings did you notice?

PRAYER:

Father, I'm learning that You don't require me to run on "empty." You know what nourishes my soul and makes me laugh. Will You help me do some of those things this week?

DAY FOUR:

Forgiveness

Take heart, son; your sins are forgiven.
—Matthew 9:2b

Therefore I tell you, whatever you ask for in prayer, believe that you have received it, and it will be yours. And when you stand praying, if you hold anything against anyone, forgive him, so that your Father in heaven may forgive you your sins.
—Mark 11:24-25

BEFORE YOU BEGIN:

- Pray. Ask God to quiet your mind and help you listen to His voice.
- Determine to be gut-level honest in your responses.
- Commit yourself to the Lord's healing process for you.

QUESTIONS:

1. Unmet expectations, adoption realities, compromised beginnings, wounds, detours, alternate routes, grief, and loss . . . words that mark our journeys. They also point to fractured relationships and shattered dreams. Under that pile of refuse lie hurts, pain, and unresolved issues. What we choose to do about forgiving those who have hurt us or our children lies at the core of our bondage or freedom! Take time to reflect on your adoption journey: how it started, who traveled with you, who didn't you thought should have, who hurt you, who hurt your child, etc. Ask God to show you who He wants you to forgive. Write those names or initials below:

2. Look back to the section entitled "Forgiveness," and review the forgiveness steps listed there. Identify and record where you are in that process:

3. Take the next step. Check here when you've completed that step: _____.

4. Write a letter of forgiveness to your child, his/her birth parents, or other person God is nudging you to forgive (remember, it may be yourself!):

NOTICING:

What physical reactions and feelings did you notice?

PRAYER:

Thank You for forgiving me. Father, release me from the prison my un-forgiveness created, as I learn to forgive others as You have forgiven me.

WEEKLY SUMMARY AND MEETING

Insights, Thoughts, Comments, and Questions from Reading and Daily Exercises:

How God met me this week:

Support Group Meeting Notes:

WEEK SIX:
Right Into His Arms

Let us examine our ways and test them,
and let us return to the LORD.
—Lamentations 3:40

Adoption collisions impact all areas of life, and numerous relationships; our relationship with God cannot emerge unaffected. Feelings and coping strategies vary when faced with grief, challenges, and our own wounds. Some of us isolate ourselves for a variety of reasons, such as pride (the perfect picture we've tried to portray is about to crumble), shame (I should be able to do a better job at this), or simply to grieve. Others may over-spiritualize. Most of us, however, run ourselves ragged trying to fix problems or escape from them. Either way, we distort God's character, and our hearts remain unfulfilled, longing for more. This longing may lead to a crossroad in our faith journey, as it did for Nikki. Or, you may take more time to begin healing, as did Shannon. Take hope! A path leads to the place we do belong . . . right into our Father's arms.

Nikki's Story

"URGENT! I am at a crossroads in my faith. I can choose to move forward or retreat the way I came. I know no decision is really a decision to retreat." Nikki's journal entry, made on a day she learned more troubling information about her teenage daughter, clearly framed her options. "I felt panicked," she shared, "and realized I would either slide into victimization, or choose to take God at His word. Both felt scary to me, but I knew I wanted to trust God. Though it hasn't been easy, little by little I'm learning there are no programs, instruction manuals, or magic bullets out there . . . and that's OK." Nikki loves her daughter, but felt swallowed by her drama. Nikki defined her personal worth in terms of how her daughter turned out, and that wasn't looking too good! She knew God loved her, but she ached to experience it.

Nikki and Tim, parents of three biological sons, adopted Kylie from an African country when she was four years old. Nikki loved their busy lives filled with sporting events and outdoor activities. She envisioned a daughter nestling into their lifestyle, but adding a dimension Nikki missed. "My heart longed for a mother-daughter relationship. I hoped my daughter would be a lifelong friend, like the relationship I enjoy with my own mother. When Kylie's negative behaviors turned our lives upside down, not only did that never happen, other relationships also suffered. The unrelenting chaos at home strained our marriage; the boys felt lost when all attention shifted to Kylie. I was embarrassed each time the principal called from school. How could I explain her lying, stealing, and poor grades when I didn't understand it myself?"

The growing isolation Nikki felt eventually affected her relationship with God. "I felt unworthy. I thought I had failed God and my family because I wasn't a good enough mom. My world shrank. I begged God to change my daughter. When that didn't happen, I felt like a miserable Christian, too. Not only did I fail as a mom, I couldn't even pray right!" Nikki knew something had to change. Since her daughter seemed unlikely to change, she determined it would have to be herself.

"Once I came to the end of my 'trying,' I began my journey back to God's arms. The journey has taken several years," said Nikki. "My daughter still flounders, but I've learned I don't have to go there with her; my experience can be separate from hers. Through listening prayer I learned to identify lies I had believed. I asked God to replace them with His truth. I am a new creation in Christ! In short, I'm learning about the 'Great Exchange' God offers us. I can exchange my feelings for His Word, my script of how life should go for God's Script, my weakness for His strength. I guess what I'm saying is I'm allowing God to be my Father. I'm beginning to find the peace, rest, and acceptance that eluded me for so many years."

Nikki and Tim have little contact with their daughter, who left home as a young adult. The dream of a close mother-daughter relationship evaporated. "That still feels like a loss to me," Nikki said, "but I've grieved and accepted it. I know her life is better than if we had not adopted her. I'm still hopeful for some sort of reconciliation. But, even if it doesn't happen, I'm thankful. God used that crossroads in my life to draw me into His arms. I know I can safely leave my daughter in His hands."

—*Nikki and Tim, adoptive parents of a four-year-old from Africa.*

Shannon's Story

"We didn't acknowledge our five-story fall until we finally hit the ground ourselves, and said 'something is not right in this picture.' That's when we began trying to figure out what in the world really happened to our child, and what we needed to do to get us all off the pavement," said Shannon. " Our child was neglected, and probably an addict and fetal alcohol baby. Although her birth mother said she was clean during pregnancy, her lifestyle didn't match her words. Our daughter was cared for by her three- and four-year-old brothers before we adopted her as a toddler. She probably spent most of her life in a closet. I think this early maltreatment set Lauren up for a lot of insecurity and fear about what would happen to her."

Lauren's unmanaged fear and insecurity escalated into challenging behaviors as she grew up, creating unexpected difficulties for Shannon and Michael. They struggled to survive through shattered dreams and a stressed marriage. "At some point, I found it easier to no longer try changing her odd behaviors," Shannon said. "Instead, I developed coping mechanisms to just live with the irregularities. I became complacent, content to have no emotional relationships, as long as certain lines were not crossed. On a functional level that worked OK. But broken hearts, and the underlying tension of unresolved conflict, endured. I ended up in a place of frustration, anger, and a hardened heart. My sense of caring and empathy hit an all-time low, as I would often secretly delight in my child's woes, thinking she is getting what she deserves. These are the things you can't say to anyone—not even your spouse. This messes with your heart and your relationship with Jesus because, suddenly, you have become exactly what so frustrates you about your child—being inconsistent, two-faced, and out of control. A crisis changed our situation and forced us to move on, from just coping to healing."

Like many of us, Shannon tried to insulate herself from the rejection, loss, and guilt she felt. "I did not like being locked away and isolated from the needs and love around me," she now admits. "I started to sense that time is short, as I passed the half-century mark in life, and it caused me to consider how I really wanted to live the rest of my life. Change, for me, was necessary."

Shannon began her healing journey when she re-engaged with others and allowed her heart to be vulnerable again. "I cannot change my child, but I can change me, through the power of the Holy Spirit. As much as we want something on our own, without the Lord it is all useless. I did not like the hardened Shannon I had become. Discontentment brought me to the point of being moldable clay again, something the Lord could change and re-form. Until that softness happens, I think our best wishes are just that—best wishes. Now, I'm not as concerned about how Lauren changes, but more about how I change. I'm beginning to understand she is her own person and I am mine, and I take care of me in this equation. I think I am at a point of openness, with a true desire to move on myself. I don't know why I couldn't come to this point sooner. I guess it's just part of the journey, and one reason I want to encourage others who are in the midst of it. I try to be very open. Sometimes I share too much. But I want others to see that adoption is not an ivory tower of redemption, but a battle for the very souls of everyone involved. Adoption is a tangle of lives waiting to be woven into something beautiful, something we might see this side of heaven, or something we might have to wait for. Adoption is not an easy or righteous thing to do, and there will always be casualties. But, it still is the right thing to do, the God-thing in us, if it was His direction from the start. The logical place to be is back in His arms!"

—*Shannon and Michael, adoptive parents of a toddler through a private agency.*

Ephesians 3:14-21

My response is to get down on my knees before the Father, this magnificent Father who parcels out all heaven and earth. I ask him to strengthen you by his Spirit—not a brute strength but a glorious inner strength—that Christ will live in you as you open the door and invite him in. And I ask him that with both feet planted firmly on love, you'll be able to take in with all followers of Jesus the extravagant dimensions of Christ's love. Reach out and experience the breadth! Test its length! Plumb the depths! Rise to the heights! Live full lives, full in the fullness of God.

God can do anything, you know—far more than you could ever imagine or guess or re-

quest in your wildest dreams! He does it not by pushing us around but by working within
us, his Spirit deeply and gently within us.
—Ephesians 3:14-20, MSG

God's relentless invitation to return to His arms defies programs, formulas, rules, or acronyms. Our extravagant inheritance as Christians on earth is to live full lives, bursting with the fullness of God . . . separate from, and not dependent upon, the outcomes of our children with challenges.

The following tools may help us grow in our experience of living this inheritance; the Holy Spirit completes the work.

Right into His A.R.M.S.
Allow GOD TO BE YOUR FATHER

"I will be a Father to you, and you will be my sons and daughters,
says the Lord Almighty."
—2 Corinthians 6:18

Viewing God as our "heavenly Father" is one thing. Allowing Him to be a Father is quite another. One view keeps Him perched a safe distance away in heaven, the other surrenders access to our heart. Isn't this the same challenge our children face when we adopt them?

Kelly adopted a two-year-old boy from South America. While he grew up, she never broke through his rejection of her. "What I realized," she said, "was he never allowed me to be his mom. Sure, we chose him, traveled twice to his birth country, and jumped through innumerable hoops to prove we were good enough parents, and we wanted him to be our son. Legally, I'm his mother . . . but he's never emotionally trusted me and allowed me to be his mom."

Returning to our Father's arms is a choice . . . a choice to allow God to be our Father. He has gone to extraordinary lengths demonstrating His love for us. We'll never experience the fullness of what that means until we trust His heart toward us, and allow Him to be our Abba Father.

Rely on God and throw away the programs!

Therefore, prepare your minds for action; be self-controlled; set your hope fully on the grace to be given you when Jesus Christ is revealed.
—1 Peter 1:13

Simply stated:

- **Prepare your mind for action:** We need to educate ourselves, understand the issues and costs of adoption. Adoption is emotionally expensive! Personal wounds, marital differences, stress, our children's compromised beginnings, relational challenges with birth parents, extended family issues, and chronic uncertainty, to name a few, extract costly withdrawals from our emotional bank accounts. We have access to professional help; use it! We know how we think affects our emotions, and what we feel affects our behavior. When we prepare our minds for action based on God's word and accurate information, we increase the likelihood of more successfully navigating the inevitable events life brings.

- **Be self-controlled:** God is in control! Our struggle is not against flesh and blood, but against the powers of this dark world (Ephesians 6:12). As we prepare our minds for action based on the truths of God's word, exchanging our lies for His truth, we pave the way for the Holy Spirit to heal the wounds we carry. This helps prevent exaggerated responses when our child smashes into those wounds. As we prepare our minds for action, maybe reframing the situation, we anticipate ways to exercise self-control.

- **Rely on God:** We still can't fix our child, but we can look up! Programs make us lazy. They enable us to think it's still within our power to fix ourselves and our children. Programs can lead to legalism which, by the way, looks amazingly similar to what we're struggling to free ourselves from! Be wary of pat answers and quick fixes. God does use people, skilled professionals, and books; that's great! We need all the help we can get. However, we must resist the temptation to place all our hope in them.

Make room for Sabbath rest

There remains, then, a Sabbath rest for the people of God;
for anyone who enters God's rest also rests from his own work,
just as God did from his. Let us, therefore, make every effort to enter that rest,
so that no one will fall by following their example of disobedience.
—Hebrews 4:9-11

In his book The Rest of God, Mark Buchanan makes the following comments: "God made us from dust. We're never too far from our origins. The apostle Paul says we're only clay pots—dust mixed with water, passed through fire. Hard, yes, but brittle too. Knowing this, God gave us the gift of Sabbath—not just as a day, but as an orientation, a way of seeing and knowing . . . Sabbath is both a day and an attitude to nurture such stillness. It is both time on a calendar and a disposition of the heart."

Consumed by the busyness surrounding us, we may lose touch with our own hearts. Learning to cultivate a spirit of rest, creating margin in our lives, moves us toward our Father's arms. To keep the Sabbath is "to practice, mostly through thankfulness, the presence of God until you are utterly convinced of His goodness and sovereignty, until He's bigger, and you find your rest in Him alone."

To practice the presence of God helps replace our distorted perceptions of God's character with the truth. Here, God invites us to seek Him alone.

Seek him

My heart says of you, "Seek his face!" Your face, LORD, I will seek.
—Psalm 27:8

When we take time to listen, we hear our heart's desire, and it is to seek Him! Our heart's desire is God's relentless invitation to return to His arms.

God is not limited by time or space. He knows each wound we sustained and the damage our hearts endured. He knows our broken places. He longs to heal the brokenhearted and bind up our wounds (Psalm 147:3).

When we seek Him:

- He counsels us (1 Kings 22:5).
- He helps us (Isaiah 31:1).
- He causes our hearts to rejoice (1 Chronicles 16:10-11, Psalm 40:16, Psalm 70:4).
- He will be found (1 Chronicles 28:9, Proverbs 8:17, Jeremiah 29:13-14, Acts 17:27).
- He will hear us (2 Chronicles 7:14).
- He will never forsake us (Psalm 9:10).
- He showers us with righteousness (Hosea 10:12).
- We will live! (Amos 5:4, 6, 14).
- We are blessed (Psalm 119:2).
- We will praise Him (Psalm 22:26).
- Those who seek the Lord lack no good thing (Psalm 34:10).
- He rewards those who earnestly seek Him (Hebrews 11:6).

Let's turn now to some practical applications to help us on our journey to the place we do belong . . . right into our Father's arms.

DAILY SESSIONS: WEEK SIX

Because of the LORD's great love we are not consumed, for his compassions never fail. They are new every morning; great is your faithfulness. I say to myself, "The LORD is my portion; therefore I will wait for him." The LORD is good to those whose hope is in him, to the one who seeks him; it is good to wait quietly for the salvation of the LORD.
—Lamentations 3:22-26

SOME THOUGHTS BEFORE YOU BEGIN:

- Offer yourself to the Lord each day . . . just the way you are!

- Set aside time to think about and record your answers to each day's questions.

- Ask God to quiet your heart and mind; invite Him into your process. He is the only one who truly knows you, your child, your family, and your story.

- Notice and make note of your feelings. Give yourself permission to feel the wide range of emotions certain to surface.

- Be honest . . . no over-spiritualizing, criticism, or judgment allowed.

- Give God permission to love you!

- There is no right or wrong answer. Dispense with "shoulds."

This week we'll continue adding new tools to our parenting toolbox.
We'll add: ARMS

- **A**llow God to be our Father
- **R**ely on God
- **M**ake room for Sabbath rest
- **S**eek Him

DAY ONE:

Allow God to be Your Father

"Long story short: we don't get to make our lives up. We get to receive our lives as gifts . . . Christians are people who recognize that we have a father whom we can thank for our existence. Christian discipleship is about learning to receive our lives as gifts without regret."
—Jean Vanier, *Living Gently in a Violent World*

BEFORE YOU BEGIN:

- Pray. Ask God to quiet your mind and help you listen to His voice.
- Determine to be gut-level honest in your responses.
- Commit yourself to the Lord's healing process for you.

QUESTIONS:

1. This exercise is about thanksgiving . . . not the day, but an attitude of the heart! Write your prayer to God. Thank Him for your existence, and receive your life as a gift. Be specific!

Overcoming wounds from our earthly father is generally understood to impede our ability to allow God to be a Father to us. Even the best dads fall short of the holiness of God. Some of us may have already resolved this issue. That's great! This exercise will validate all your hard work. Others have not. Let this be a gentle invitation to explore this now. Perhaps a father's death or abandonment magnified the desire for a father.

Or maybe we adapted to this loss, and believe we're self-sufficient and don't really need a father. Whatever our story, and wherever we are in it, we can experience peace, and move toward a more healthy perspective of God as a father to us.

2. What experiences or characteristics of your earthly father make it easy to embrace the fatherhood of God?

3. What experiences or characteristics of your earthly father hinder you in embracing God's invitation to be a father to you?

4. Perhaps un-forgiveness toward our fathers has become a heavy stone in our backpack. Let's pause, pull it out, name it, and lay it at the feet of Jesus. Check here when done___.

Write a letter of forgiveness to your father for those areas where he fell short. (Use additional pages as needed.)

5. Take some time to think about what Scripture tells us of God's character. What characteristics of God make Him a trustworthy father?

6. *"I will be a Father to you, and you will be my sons and daughters, says the Lord Almighty."* —2 Corinthians 6:18

Ponder your response to God's invitation. What would your life feel and look like if you allowed God to be a Father to you?

7. Draw a picture or write a poem portraying the father-daughter relationship you desire to have with God:

NOTICING:

What physical reactions and feelings did you notice?

PRAYER:

Oh Father, I do want to allow You to be a Father to me. I surrender my heart to You. I know it is safe in Your hands and You will treat it gently.

DAY TWO:

Rely on God (and throw away the programs!)

He tends his flock like a shepherd:
He gathers the lambs in his arms
and carries them close to his heart;
he gently leads those that have young.
—Isaiah 40:11

The eternal God is your refuge,
and underneath are the everlasting arms.
—Deuteronomy 33:27

BEFORE YOU BEGIN:

- Pray. Ask God to quiet your mind and help you listen to His voice.
- Determine to be gut-level honest in your responses.
- Commit yourself to the Lord's healing process for you.

QUESTIONS:

1. In what programs, books, or people have you placed your hope to fix you, your child, or your family?

Write them on a piece of paper or sticky note, one per page. One at a time, wad them up and throw them away. Tell God, out loud with each toss, you choose to place your hope in Him.

2. How can we use these books, programs, or people as useful tools, without placing our hope in them?

3. God created us for relationship . . . with one another and with Him. He provides tools and resources, but He never intended them to replace a love relationship with Himself. He created us as an expression of His love and to fulfill His purposes. He knows our brokenness, our strivings, and our failures. He watched us begin our worthy journey, knowing it would take many of us to that place we didn't belong. Wherever we are, His arms are not too short to rescue us.

Read Isaiah 40:11, Page 116. He is our shepherd. Close your eyes. Imagine what it feels like for Jesus the shepherd to gather you in His arms and hold you close to His heart. Check here when you are done_____.

Describe what you felt:

Right into His arms . . . Imagine you're on a trek. Tired and weary, you approach a crossroad with clearly-marked signs. You notice the road you've been traveling will lead to "A Place I Didn't Belong." However, a less-traveled road will take you "Right into His Arms." Both roads require more travel, and you can't see the final destination. Needing to rest, you stop, remove your backpack, and ponder the signs. You imagine what it will look and feel like if you remain on the path that brought you to this crossroad. You envision yourself, your child, your family, and your social relationships ten years from now. In order to make a good decision about which road to take, you imagine what your destination would look like if you turned off the road and headed "Right into His Arms." Refreshed from your brief stop, you gather your backpack and journey on. Which road did you take? Write it on the crossroads below:

Write your prayer to God for the journey ahead:

NOTICING:

What physical reactions and feelings did you notice?

PRAYER:

Father, I don't know what the destination looks or feels like, but I want to change the course of my journey, and take the path that leads right into Your arms.

DAY THREE:

Make Room for Sabbath Rest

Bear in mind that the LORD has given you the Sabbath;
that is why on the sixth day he gives you bread for two days.
Everyone is to stay where he is on the seventh day; no one is to go out.
So the people rested on the seventh day.
—Exodus 16:29-30

Come, let us return to the LORD. He has torn us to pieces but he
will heal us; he has injured us but he will bind up our wounds.
After two days he will revive us; and on the third day he will restore us,
that we may live in his presence. Let us acknowledge the LORD;
let us press on to acknowledge him. As surely as the sun rises,
he will appear; he will come to us like the winter rains, like the
spring rains that water the earth.
—Hosea 6:1-3

BEFORE YOU BEGIN:

- Pray. Ask God to quiet your mind and help you listen to His voice.
- Determine to be gut-level honest in your responses.
- Commit yourself to the Lord's healing process for you.

QUESTIONS:

1. Mark Buchanan states: "Sabbath is both time on a calendar and a disposition of the heart." Which of those do you feel lacking in your life? Explain your need below:

2. God created us to need rest, and to rest in Him. Our journey back to His arms will be marked by learning to rest, and creating margin in our lives. This may feel counter-intuitive to our usual busyness, and the infinite list of "shoulds" dominating our contemporary existence. In the table below, list some obstacles keeping you from entering into His rest. For example, getting the kids up, fed, bathed, dressed, changed, dressed again, and out the door on Sunday can feel like an obstacle to experiencing a day of rest. Worry or constantly planning ahead may rob us of experiencing the Sabbath as a disposition of the heart. What are your obstacles? Write them in the table below. Find one small change you want to make to remove one or two obstacles, and write it in the margin:

SABBATH: DAY OF REST	SABBATH: DISPOSITION OF THE HEART

3. Dr. Richard Swenson, in his bestselling book *Margin*, asserts most of us need rest in three areas: physical, emotional, and spiritual. He opines that spiritual rest, "though widely neglected, is of supreme importance." Write a prayer to God below painting a picture of the spiritual rest you desire. Ask Him to help you:

Listen for His voice, and then write His response here:

4. Dr. Swenson describes the following circumstances as "contemporary commotion"—things depriving us of rest. Check all items applicable to you:

_____ Noise

_____ Activity overload

_____ Inappropriate expectations

_____ Pride

_____ Discontent and covetousness

_____ Preoccupation with success

_____ Preoccupation with power

_____ Debt

_____ Our image

_____ Our reputation

_____ Fractured relationships

5. What is your response to the items you checked?

6. Review your checkmarks. Ask God to reveal what lies you believe in the midst of contemporary commotion contributing to rest deprivation. Ask Him to reveal His truth. Write your prayer to Him below, exchanging one lie for one truth:

NOTICING:

What physical reactions and feelings did you notice?

PRAYER:

Thank You, Father for creating me to need Your rest. Help me learn to keep Your day holy. Teach me to experience the spiritual posture of rest during my contemporary commotions.

DAY FOUR:

Seek Him

"You will seek me and find me when you seek me
with all your heart. I will be found by you," declares the LORD,
"and will bring you back from captivity."
—Jeremiah 29:13-14a

BEFORE YOU BEGIN:

- Pray. Ask God to quiet your mind and help you listen to His voice.
- Determine to be gut-level honest in your responses.
- Commit yourself to the Lord's healing process for you.

QUESTIONS:

1. Seek Him! Sit quietly for ten minutes. Set aside distractions as they enter your mind. Focus on Him alone. Check here when you have completed this_____.

God extends His relentless invitation to each of us. This one has your name on it!

Listen carefully as He extends His invitation to you, then write it on the invitation to the right:

NOTICING:

What physical reactions and feelings did you notice?

PRAYER:

Thank you, Father for Your relentless and personal invitation. Teach me to seek You with all my heart.

WEEKLY SUMMARY AND MEETING

Insights, Thoughts, Comments, and Questions from Reading and Daily Exercises:

How God met me this week:

Support Group Meeting Notes:

WEEK SEVEN:
Creating Healthy Support Communities

"There are three activities that are absolutely vital in the creation of community. The first is eating together around the table. The second is praying together. And the third is celebrating together. By celebrating, I mean to laugh, to fool around, to have fun, to give thanks together for life."
—Jean Vanier

Now that we've embraced our crossroad experience, and chosen to continue on our journey right into His arms, we'll allow this new perspective to guide our thoughts and feelings while we consider the state of our marriage and support systems. When "support" relationships drain us as much as our kids do (withdrawals from our emotional bank account!), it's time to reconsider our banking strategy. This week, we'll identify common relational threats, and consider ways to strengthen our marriage, prepare family and friends, and build our team to help sustain us for the journey.

Ginny's Story

Ginny expected a wonderful journey into the sunset with the man of her dreams when she married. At first, things clipped along according to plan. Ginny and Mark enjoyed being together, and agreed on most things. What disagreements they had, however, lingered for days while Ginny withdrew into a tailspin. "As the years passed, we both matured in our ability to handle dissenting opinions within the marriage," Ginny shared. "We could normally reconcile before the end of the day. Having worked so hard to get our marriage into a safe and comfortable relationship, I was not prepared for the trauma the relationship would endure under the attack of a challenging adopted child."

Ginny and Mark decided to adopt after having three biological daughters. Moved by the plight of orphans around the world, they knew they had lots of love to share with a child. Their spiritual and moral convictions motivated them to adopt internationally. "We added child number four to our family by adopting our youngest daughter. Life went into overdrive, with four kids under the age of five at home. Mark and I no longer saw eye to eye. That caused me to question everything I did as a wife and mom; running away seemed like a valid option at the time. Physically I never made it out the door; emotionally I became very withdrawn and uncommunicative. Mark traveled a lot back then. He once asked me if I really could take care of the kids—if they would be safe, if I would be here, really here, when he returned."

Shaken by Mark's doubts, Ginny pulled herself together enough to put on a game face for a few more years, and then everything completely unraveled. "The issues with our adopted child became more pronounced, as did 'friendly advice' from others. I saw our child differently than Mark did, and felt he just didn't want to, or couldn't, see what was really happening in our home. A chasm developed between Mark and me and, for a few minutes, I stopped my pity party and got really mad. I was not going to let a child come between me and my husband. I felt jealous and enraged. That's when I knew I was broken enough to seek help for my child." Ginny and Mark wisely sought counseling for themselves, as well. "Under the guidance of a good counselor and the Word of God, I began to see I was OK, and do have value. Mark realized how he let our child manipulate him, and let her come between us. We promised one another to never let a child come between us again. We would stick together as a united front, turning first to one another for information, feedback, and enlightenment."

Things have not been easy for Ginny and Mark. They recognize their daughters are young, and many active parenting years lie ahead of them. They have, however, overcome the divisiveness which marked their marriage following the adoption of a child with challenges. "We developed strategies to check with one another on all things, to not answer any question without first checking with the other parent, and to hold all discussions with our child as a couple," Ginny shared. "A simple request for a date is immediately answered, and we are out the door for 'couple time!' And, yes, we have learned to disagree without the world falling apart. We have also learned we can withstand anything we choose to face together."

—*Ginny and Mark, adoptive parents of an infant from Asia.*

Annie's Story

Quiet filled the house. The kids were back at school after a Christmas break that dragged a couple of days too long. Late for work, Dan had swish-kissed her good-bye, grabbed a bagel, and rushed out the door. Annie sighed, savoring her solitude. Breakfast dishes piled high in the kitchen sink could wait. Annie poured a second cup of coffee and slipped away to her quiet place. As the fading holiday season wrapped her in memories, she looked back with thanksgiving at how her life had changed over the past year. A butterfly held captive in her cocoon, Annie recently had emerged as a beautiful butterfly. Oh, the difference perspective makes!

Annie settled into her favorite chair, gathered months of journals on her lap, and began reading. "I've spent years feeling lonely. Misunderstood. I am happily married. I mean, our marriage isn't perfect, not by a long shot, but I'm sure glad I married Dan! But, as far as feeling known and understood goes—now that's a toughy. Dan is good, but I rarely feel known and understood in friendships or with people at church. That gap widened even further after we adopted the boys. I'm finally a mom. So why do I have so little in common with other moms in my world? They don't understand, or even like, my kids. I feel like they just want to fix the boys . . . or me. My extended family isn't much different. I know they want to love our children, but I sure get a lot of criticism from them. That hurts. I'm sad, but it's just easier not to try to fit in. I still feel so lonely."

Tears sprang to her eyes as she absorbed the sadness of those words. Annie let herself linger in the memory before continuing on and coming to this entry: "I met a friend today! Maybe God really does answer prayers. Mary is also an adoptive mom, whose sixteen-year-old daughter was just diagnosed with fetal alcohol spectrum disorder. Wow. I can't imagine what that would be like. Anyway, it was great to visit with her. I just knew she understood me better than anyone I've known before. Maybe there are more Mary's out there!"

Morning melted into afternoon as Annie continued reading. She sensed the change within herself as one entry after another chronicled her journey. Her safety network grew. She got involved in projects outside the home demanding time and creativity. Her perspective slowly changed, from looking inward to gazing outward. She read through notes from an adoption conference she attended. Sitting in the room with other adoptive families, she identified with the speaker's description of life as an adoptive family. People she barely knew felt like kin. Her journal entry the following day read: "After that, I realized I was not crazy. I was not alone. People who understood really existed."

Annie noticed she shared less with old friends, holding her cards close to her chest around them. At the same time, she began testing the waters with people who seemed to understand. When she felt safe, knowing they might also have experiential understanding of her world, she opened up. As she read her most recent entry, the smile lighting her face melted into her heart. "I love the new adoption support group I've been attending. There, I found the most wonderful women who understand, encourage, and inspire me—God's kind provision again. I realize I continue to make progress on this journey. Little by little. I am blessed now to have a number of friends who 'get it' and with whom I can talk about life filter-free. I have come to a beautiful place. Walking this road is not easy, but it is so much better with these sojourners."

The butterfly had emerged!

—*Annie and Dan, adoptive parents of pre-school-aged twin boys from foster care.*

RELATIONAL D.I.G.S.

> *Has not the LORD made them one? In flesh and spirit they are his. And why one?*
> *Because he was seeking godly offspring. So guard yourself in your spirit,*
> *and do not break faith with the wife of your youth.*
> —Malachi 2:15

We know marriages frequently take a hit when we parent children with challenges. However, that does not change the fact God intends marriage to be the most intimate relationship we experience on earth. The two become one when we enter into this covenant. One reason is to produce godly offspring. Satan understands this, and conspires to undermine our efforts. Ineffective ways of dealing with wounds, and the stressors our children bring, threaten to unravel our oneness when we need it most. We should expect and prepare for the following D.I.G.S. on our marriage, and in other supportive relationships, when we parent children with challenges.

Divide and Conquer

*Be self-controlled and alert. Your enemy the devil prowls
around like a roaring lion looking for someone to devour.*
—1 Peter 5:8

Take a moment to flip back to Week Four, A Place I Didn't Belong. The section entitled "Mom as Target" helps us understand, from our child's perspective, why it's important to ensure he or she doesn't have another mother. Many children intuitively believe they would not survive the loss of another mom; they invest emotional energy to reject such love, as if their lives depend on it! As dire as that outcome might seem, the potential of even graver consequences may exist.

If Satan creates or exacerbates a wedge between husband and wife, he has dismantled and disarmed God's design for creating godly offspring. Dad frequently doesn't understand the battle waging for his child's heart. He may succumb to temptation, and think his wife may be a tad-bit crazy. He could seek temporary peace, at his wife's expense, instead of oneness with her. Perhaps mom views dad as the "enemy" when he fails to validate her experience. The unrelenting demands, chaos, and drama in our homes suck precious life and energy from us. We sometimes don't know when to say "no" in trying to meet those demands; unwittingly, we conspire to sabotage our marriage. When either partner fails to identify threats to marital oneness and take corrective action, they comply with Satan's plan; when Satan divides, he conquers.

Isolation

*Let us not give up meeting together, as some are in the habit of doing, but let us
encourage one another—and all the more as you see the Day approaching.*
—Hebrews 10:25

Heather Forbes and Sophia Dziegielewski, in their 2003 article "Issues Facing Adoptive Mothers of Children with Special Needs" (*Journal of Social Work*), cite research suggesting many Americans still consider adoption second best to becoming parents by birth. They suggest this notion developed in the 1940s, when adoption practice focused on the adoptive mother rather than the child. Practitioners believed an infertile mother did not have the capacity to love an adopted child, and was somehow inferior as a woman. This implied an adopted child's problems correlated to mom's lack of self-acceptance, unrealistic expectations, and hostility toward the child.

In 2000, two-thirds of adoptive moms surveyed stated they felt negatively impacted by the prevailing belief of adoptive motherhood as inferior. Forbes and Dziegielewski further noted that, in a research study they conducted, 79 percent of adoptive moms with special needs kids felt isolated in their struggles, hurt by the lack of support they received, ostracized outside of their immediate families, and had lost friends because of the adoption.

Additionally, ineffective help for adoptive parents of children with challenges often leads to feelings of isolation. Some parents believe asking for help means they have failed; they fear others may view them as inadequate parents. Friends can't relate to our situation. In our quest for services, many adoptive parents end up educating the professionals who are supposed to help us. Therapists, in turn, often blame parents for the child's behavior. Continually bumping into walls of misunderstanding, incompetence, and blame contributes to our sense of isolation. When we feel isolated, relationships suffer.

Scriptural references to isolation generally speak of putting or keeping an infected person in isolation to keep disease from spreading, or to isolate mildew. Isolation for people is not good! Throughout Scripture, God paints a picture of community. He is three in one. He declared in Genesis that it was not good for man to be alone; husband and wife together reflect God's glory. He sets the solitary in families. He tells us not to forsake the assembling together of believers. Where two or more are gathered, He is there with us. God hardwires us for community. We need to surround ourselves with communities which include us, and don't treat us as though we're infected! When we feel isolated, it behooves us to examine, improve, or change our support communities.

God Loves the Orphan

A father to the fatherless, a defender of widows, is God in his holy dwelling.
God sets the lonely in families,
—Psalm 68:5-6a

Scripture is very clear, God loves the orphan! He protects the fatherless. He is their helper, their father, and their defender. He sustains them. He has compassion for them. With arms outstretched, Jesus invites the children to come to Him. God warns us to not take advantage of an orphan, or deprive the fatherless of justice. We're responsible for defending the cause of the weak. As we grow closer to God, our love for orphans may intensify. Some respond by welcoming one (or more!) children into their homes through adoption.

The flip side of this coin, however, is equally true. Satan hates the orphan, because they are near to our Father's heart. He opposes any means whereby children are saved in this world for the next. Simply by loving orphans, we open the door to spiritual warfare and conflict in our homes. Beware! Satan intends to divide, conquer, and isolate us to thwart God's redemptive plan.

Stress

Consider it pure joy, my brothers, whenever you face trials of many kinds, because you know that the testing of your faith develops perseverance. Perseverance must finish its work so that you may be mature and complete, not lacking anything. If any of you lacks wisdom, he should ask God, who gives generously to all without finding fault, and it will be given to him.
—James 1:2-5

COGNITIVE:	EMOTIONAL:
Memory problems	Moodiness
Inability to concentrate	Irritability
Poor judgment	Unable to relax
Negative attitude	Overwhelmed
Anxious thoughts	Loneliness or isolation
Worry	Depression
PHYSICAL:	**BEHAVIORAL:**
Aches and pains	Eating more or less
Diarrhea or constipation	Sleeping too much or too little
Nausea	Isolating
Chest pain	Procrastination
Rapid heartbeat	Use of alcohol or drugs to help relax
Loss of sex drive	Nervous habits (nail biting, etc.)
Frequent colds	

Got stress? Of course you do! We may not be able to define it, but we all know what stress feels like. Our busy lives overflow with stress. Stress has become so commonplace, it is accepted as a way of life. While not all stress is bad, when we constantly operate in pedal-to-the-metal mode, our minds and bodies suffer; so do our relationships! Take a look at the list of warning signs of stress on the previous page, and identify which ones you've experienced.

The cause of our stress depends largely upon our perception of events in our lives. Think back to our earlier discussion of the thought/behavior diagram:

Event ⇨ Thought ⇨ Feeling ⇨ Behavior

How we think about an event affects our feelings and behavior toward it. While stress remains subjective in origin, we all experience both external and internal stressors. Examples include:

EXTERNAL:	INTERNAL:
Major life changes	Perfectionism
Children and family	Unrealistic expectations
Relationship difficulties	Pessimistic attitude
Finances	Inability to accept uncertainty
Too busy!	

Our support networks, sense of control, attitude and outlook on life, ability to manage our emotions, and our knowledge and preparation all influence our ability to tolerate stress. Choosing to apply biblical truth (consider it pure joy!) may mitigate emotional and behavioral responses to stress. Subjecting ourselves to long-term or chronic stress leads to serious health problems. As we improve our ability to manage relational stress, our whole body will thank us!

A Proactive Response

- **Seek professional help** for yourself, your marriage, and your children. When we parent children with challenges, we benefit from the opportunity to allow other members of the body of Christ to exercise their gifts and talents for God's glory.

- **Adoption education:** Seek early and often for best results! Research local resources for seminars, webinars, and conferences. Attend or start an adoption support group. Read books, articles, and blogs. Commit to being a lifelong learner.

- **Parenting breaks:** For married couples or singles . . . without the kiddos! Focus on what you enjoy, and limit scheduling or problem-solving. Take this break away from home, if possible, so you won't be tempted to throw in a load of laundry, unload the dishwasher, or pay bills. Carve out time to play and nurture supportive friendships. Write it on your calendar and keep the date!

- **Pray** as a couple. This strengthens oneness and defeats isolation. Pray with a group of like-minded friends. Several years ago a group of mom-friends and I gathered each Friday morning for three years, to pray for our teenagers. We each had special concerns and guarded where we shared our stories. These four women became a lifeline of support for me, and saved the life of one of my children. God's arm is not too short to rescue you from any situation!

- **Just say no** to things screaming for your time, but offering nothing in return.

- **Make marriage a priority.** If you are married, let it show in your attitude and schedule. This creates security for our children, and helps guard against triangulation and manipulation. We need the strength and support a healthy marriage provides. Plus, as consuming as it may feel right now, hands-on parenting is generally a short season in our lives together.

As moms of children with challenges, learning to build a supportive team becomes essential to our health and well-being. Building this team may require a discerning spirit, and commitment to change or re-prioritize our relationships. Our team begins in our family and expands to include extended family members and friendships. The following daily exercises take us through a proactive examination of existing relationships, and offer tools to enhance our support community and build our team.

DAILY SESSIONS: WEEK SEVEN

*Two are better than one, because they have a good return for their
work: If one falls down, his friend can help him up. But pity the man
who falls and has no one to help him up! Also, if two lie down together, they will keep warm. But how can one keep warm alone?
Though one may be overpowered, two can defend themselves.
A cord of three strands is not quickly broken.*
—Ecclesiastes 4:9-12

SOME THOUGHTS BEFORE YOU BEGIN:

- Offer yourself to the Lord each day . . . just the way you are!

- Set aside time to think about and record your answers to each day's questions.

- Ask God to quiet your heart and mind; invite Him into your process. He is the only one who truly knows you, your child, your family, and your story.

- Notice and make note of your feelings. Give yourself permission to feel the wide range of emotions certain to surface.

- Be honest . . . no over-spiritualizing, criticism, or judgment allowed.

- Give God permission to love you!

- There is no right or wrong answer. Dispense with "shoulds."

This week we'll continue adding new tools to our parenting toolbox. We'll add:

- D.I.G.S.
- Cultivating Support
- Building a Team

DAY ONE:

Building Our House

The wise woman builds her house,
but with her own hands the foolish one tears hers down.
—Proverbs 14:1

Today's session provides an opportunity to consider the state of our oneness in marriage as we continue our journey and identify changes we can make to build our houses and strengthen our marriage.

BEFORE YOU BEGIN:

- Pray. Ask God to quiet your mind and help you listen to His voice.
- Determine to be gut-level honest in your responses.
- Commit yourself to the Lord's healing process for you.

QUESTIONS:

1. As adoptive moms of children with challenges, consider the four threats listed below. How have each impacted your marriage? You might want to cite examples of incidents, or methods of dealing with conflict you've developed. Then list any additional threats you have noticed.

    a. **Divide and Conquer**

    b. **Isolation**

    c. **God Loves the Orphan/Satan Hates the Orphan**

    d. **Stress**

THREAT	IMPACT
Divide and Conquer	
Isolation	
God loves the orphan	
Stress	
Other	

2. Review your answers in light of the following proactive responses:

    a. Seek professional help

    b. Adoption education

    c. Regular time together

    d. Pray

    e. Just say no!

    f. Make your marriage a priority

What changes can you make?

What changes do you want to make?

What changes do you have the energy and vision to make this week?

3. Husbands and wives generally develop different coping strategies for managing stress. Some husbands may become emotionally missing in action. Take a few moments to reflect on the different ways you and your husband perceive and manage stress. If you are married, and if you feel comfortable doing so, ask your husband to participate in answering the following questions:

a. What do you perceive as stress?

b. What does your husband perceive as stress?

c. How do you manage stress?

d. How does your husband manage stress?

e. What conflicts have these differences created?

f. Schedule a time this week to share and discuss these insights with your husband. Check here when completed ___.

g. What did God reveal to you through this communication?

4. Write a letter to your husband, if married, expressing your need and desire for oneness.

___ Check here when you complete the letter.
___ Check here if you shared the letter with your spouse.

NOTICING:

What physical reactions and feelings did you notice?

PRAYER:

Oh Father, thank You for not making us travel this journey alone. You are with us. Help us experience the oneness You created for us. Thank You that a cord of three strands is not easily broken!

DAY TWO:
Extended Family Members

Praise be to the God and Father of our Lord Jesus Christ, the Father of compassion and the God of all comfort, who comforts us in all our troubles, so that we can comfort those in any trouble with the comfort we ourselves have received from God. For just as the sufferings of Christ flow over into our lives, so also through Christ our comfort overflows.
—2 Corinthians 1:3-5

Learning to cultivate support within our family is vitally important. This includes other children in our home, as well as extended family members such as grandparents, aunts, uncles, cousins, etc. Open communication, bathed in grace, eases the way. When we include family members, and help prepare and educate them, it can ease fears and create some of our greatest fans.

BEFORE YOU BEGIN:

- Pray. Ask God to quiet your mind and help you listen to His voice.
- Determine to be gut-level honest in your responses.
- Commit yourself to the Lord's healing process for you.

QUESTIONS:

1. Other children in the home often suffer the greatest consequences when their parents adopt children with challenges. They may lose their place in the birth order, or simply struggle with the demands the new child makes on a strained family system. Children observe and question differences in discipline. They may feel "lost" in the crowd, and seek acceptance outside the family circle. If you have other children in the home, identify the potential impact your adoption had on them.

2. Pick a time this week to begin or continue a conversation with these other children. Ask open-ended questions. Listen and don't interrupt. Resist the urge to defend yourself or their adopted sibling. Ask forgiveness if appropriate. Listen to their heart. What did it say?

3. Grandparents carry their own wounds, as well as those we inflict on them! Adoption may not be how they dreamed of becoming grandparents. While they will undoubtedly embrace the new child in the family, they, too, may need to recognize and grieve their loss of a biological grandchild. Consider their story. What might their losses include? Write a letter to your parents or your in-laws expressing your understanding of their loss:

Check here when done _____.

4. Grandparents will do best if you include them from the outset. Let them know what you're thinking, and be prepared to answer pragmatic questions. While the final decision lies with you, they most likely have your best interest at heart. Validate their concerns, and seek to nurture a healthy adoptive environment from the start. Allow them to grow into acceptance at their own rate—which requires working through grief and personal values about adoption.

Consider how this happened or didn't happen in your family. Looking back, what did you do well in helping to cultivate their support? What could you have done better? Knowing it's never too late, pray and ask God what steps He would like to help you take with your parents or in-laws.

5. Everyone's opinion in the family is not the same! You value some more than others. List ten family members below. Number them from one to ten, beginning with the person whose opinion you value most. Begin there with the next question.

6. What are some ways you can include, prepare, or educate extended family members you want on your support team?

NOTICING:

What physical reactions and feelings did you notice?

PRAYER:

Thank you, Father, that, in Your sovereignty, You placed me in my family. You know our strengths and weaknesses. Help me be a vessel of reconciliation. Give our parents open hearts and minds to understand.

DAY THREE:

The Faith of a Few Close Friends

Some men came, bringing to him a paralytic, carried by four of them.
Since they could not get him to Jesus because of the crowd, they made
an opening in the roof above Jesus and, after digging through it, lowered
the mat the paralyzed man was lying on. When Jesus saw their faith, he
said to the paralytic, "Son, your sins are forgiven."
—Mark 2:3-5

BEFORE YOU BEGIN:

- Pray. Ask God to quiet your mind and help you listen to His voice.
- Determine to be gut-level honest in your responses.
- Commit yourself to the Lord's healing process for you.

QUESTIONS:

1. Read and contemplate Jean Vanier's quote at the beginning of this chapter. He identifies three activities vital to creating community: eating together, praying together, and celebrating together. Consider the relationships listed at the left of the table on the following page, then jot down your evaluation in the columns to the right.

	EATING TOGETHER	PRAYING TOGETHER	CELEBRATING
Marriage			
Other children in home			
Grown children			
Grandparents			
Other extended family members			
Friends from home			
Current friends			
Neighborhood friends			
Church friends			
Spiritual leaders/ mentors			
Job relationships			

Now review your response. What insights do you have?

2. Evaluate your current support systems (family, friends, church, neighborhood, job, etc.).

    a. Who are those you can't or don't want to share your true story with, and why?

    b. Who *do* you feel comfortable sharing your story with, and why?

    c. Make a list of friends and family members who nurture you. Which of their traits are most helpful and life-giving to you?

NURTURING FAMILY AND FRIENDS	HELPFUL, LIFE-GIVING TRAITS

d. Consider your responses. Which relationships are withdrawals from your emotional bank account? Which ones do you consider deposits?

WITHDRAWALS	DEPOSITS

e. What changes might you need to make in your banking strategy? How will you make these changes?

3. Write a prayer to God telling Him your response to His provisions, the insights you gained, and your needs in this area.

NOTICING:

What physical reactions and feelings did you notice?

PRAYER:

Thank you, Father, for the faith of a few close friends. Help me be that to others who need Your comfort.

DAY FOUR:

Team Building!

From him the whole body, joined and held together by every supporting
ligament, grows and builds itself up in love, as each part does its work.
—Ephesians 4:16

BEFORE YOU BEGIN:

- Pray. Ask God to quiet your mind and help you listen to His voice.
- Determine to be gut-level honest in your responses.
- Commit yourself to the Lord's healing process for you.

QUESTIONS:

When we take time to evaluate our support systems, we open the door to new opportunities. While we can't change our parents, and probably won't change our spouse, there are many changes we can make to cultivate a nurturing support team. Who knows, we might even be the answer to someone else's prayers! We all need fellowship and a place to belong.

1. How would you feel and act if you knew you were completely understood and supported within your various communities (family, church, neighborhood, job, etc.)?

2. Write your prayer to God. Thank Him if you experience this. Ask Him to meet that need if it's not yet real. Expect Him to answer beyond anything you can think or imagine.

3. How can you be that friend to another mom of children with challenges? What do you have to offer? Pray, listen, and write the name of that person below:

NOTICING:

What physical reactions and feelings did you notice?

PRAYER:

Father, I believe You will help create supportive communities in my life. Show me whose team I can be on! I want to offer that back to You.

WEEKLY SUMMARY AND MEETING

Insights, Thoughts, Comments, and Questions from Reading and Daily Exercises:

How God met me this week:

Support Group Meeting Notes:

WEEK EIGHT:
Glancing Back, Pressing Forward

*I'm not saying that I have this all together, that I have it made. But I
am well on my way, reaching out for Christ, who has so wondrously
reached out for me. Friends, don't get me wrong: by no means do I count
myself an expert in all of this, but I've got my eye on the goal, where
God is beckoning us onward—to Jesus. I'm off and running, and I'm not
turning back. So let's keep focused on that goal, those of us who want
everything God has for us. If any of you have something else in mind,
something less than total commitment, God will clear your blurred vision—you'll see it yet! Now that we're on the right track, let's stay on it.*
—Philippians 3:12-16, MSG

My Dear Friend,

What an incredible journey we've shared these past weeks. I pray God has met you
wherever you are in your adoption experience, and you have reclaimed hope for your
journey . . . even if it's just a glimmer.

Glancing Back

In a spirit of grace we considered the role our adoption expectations and realities
played in how we experienced our adoption journey. We learned how our child's compromised beginning, and the wounds we carry, collided with expectations, and delivered each of us to a place we didn't belong. Although unrelenting pain fills that pit stop,
we know it's not a final destination! Our determination to get back on track allowed us

to receive new tools for living, such as: identifying and tending to our wounds; caring for ourselves; forgiving others; allowing God to be a Father to us; relying on God; making room for Sabbath rest; seeking Him; and proactively preparing, educating, and cultivating our support systems. We know there are no programs or quick fixes to replace the power of hope in a God who specializes in transforming and redeeming broken lives.

In many ways, *A Place I Didn't Belong* chronicles my efforts to adjust, heal, and reclaim hope on my adoption journey. I've also talked with enough of "us" along the way to know I'm not alone. I'm grateful beyond words for each woman who entrusted her sacred story to me and allowed me to share it here. Thank you.

I never intended for this to be a Bible study, to exclude those who don't share my faith, or suggest there is only one way back to our Father's arms. I wanted simply to:

- Validate your experience;
- Help create safe communities for adoptive moms of children with challenges;
- Point you to Jesus, the Wonderful Counselor;
- Share some tools for living; and,
- Help you reclaim hope for your adoption journey.

If any of these has been accomplished, praise God. To the extent I've inhibited your healing process, I ask your forgiveness.

Pressing Forward

So, where do we go from here? We took time to glance back in order to understand how we ended up at a place we didn't belong. Hopefully, we now see that place in our rearview mirror, and recognize it as the place where God began His healing work in us, so we could press forward with renewed hope.

As we bring this season to a close, hopes and wishes for you, your children, and your families flood my heart. My only response is to get down on my knees before the Father and pray you:

- Will know in the deepest part of your soul you'll be OK, no matter what happens with your children;
- Feel empowered to parent the children God entrusted to you;
- Allow God to make you worthy of His call;
- Experience His peace through the challenges;

- Rely on the strength of the Holy Spirit;
- Continue to disarm lies, and replace them with God's truth;
- Discover and experience His freedom, grace, and love;
- Feel different, even when your days look the same;
- Let the cross define your worth and identity;
- Rediscover your dreams, and make time to have fun;
- Treat yourself with grace;
- Find those people you can laugh, fool around, and share life with; and,
- Experience His blessing beyond measure.

But, most of all, I pray God continues to lead you right into His arms!

Closing Remarks

My three-year-old granddaughter and her mother currently live with us. Unsaddled from the parenting role, I'm free to just be my granddaughter's Mimi. We love to read books together and share long snuggles; she seldom tires of hearing how much I love her.

"Pst, Jada, come here," I whisper, motioning for her to join me in my chair after dinner. "Mimi has a secret for you." She squirms to free herself from the booster chair holding her prisoner, and scrambles to my side. Knowing what's to come, she giggles, climbs up on my lap, cocks her head, and waits. As I allow her anticipation to build, I lean toward her, cup my hand around her ear, and whisper, "pspspspsps . . . I love you!" Her eyes sparkle. She giggles and quickly turns her head so I can repeat the message in her other ear. "Pspspsps . . . I love you!" More giggles erupt as she clutches my face between chubby fingers and "whispers" her secret in my ear. This game continues until one of us wears out—usually me.

Our Father never wears out or tires of whispering His love song to us! As you reclaim hope, plan your course, and press forward on your adoption journey, make time to rest on His lap, near His heart, engulfed in His arms, and listen to the song He's written just for you!

With Deep Affection,
Paula

DAILY SESSIONS: WEEK EIGHT

He who has ears let him hear.
—Matthew 11:15

Trust in the LORD with all your heart
and lean not on your own understanding;
In all your ways acknowledge him,
and he will make your paths straight.
—Proverbs 3:5-6

SOME THOUGHTS BEFORE YOU BEGIN:

- Offer yourself to the Lord each day . . . just the way you are!

- Set aside time to think about and record your answers to each day's questions.

- Ask God to quiet your heart and mind; invite Him into your process. He is the only one who truly knows you, your child, your family, and your story.

- Notice and make note of your feelings. Give yourself permission to feel the wide range of emotions certain to surface.

- Be honest . . . no over-spiritualizing, criticism, or judgment allowed.

- Give God permission to love you!

- There is no right or wrong answer. Dispense with "shoulds."

This week, as we glance back, we'll dust off three tools in our toolbox that will help us press forward:

- Ears to Hear
- Heart to Understand
- Voice to Speak

DAY ONE:

Ears to Hear

My son, pay attention to what I say;
listen closely to my words.
Do not let them out of your sight,
keep them within your heart;
for they are life to those who find them
and health to a man's whole body.
—Proverbs 4:20-22

BEFORE YOU BEGIN:

- Pray. Ask God to quiet your mind and help you listen to His voice.
- Determine to be gut-level honest in your responses.
- Commit yourself to the Lord's healing process for you.

QUESTIONS:

This week, we'll spend most of our daily session times in reflection. Don't use this as an excuse to cut the time short! This may be the best work we do. Settle in with your notebook; indulge yourself with a cup of tea or a second shot of coffee. Take your time, and read back through your journal entries from the past weeks. Ask the Holy Spirit to highlight the lessons He has for you. Expect God to show up; wait for Him. Check here when you complete this step ___.

1. What lessons or insights seem most significant to you?

2. What resistance did you notice? For example, did you consistently not answer certain types of questions?

3. What patterns did you see emerge? What do you think God is telling you through this?

NOTICING:

What physical reactions and feelings did you notice?

PRAYER:

Thank you, Father, for traveling this journey with me the first time, and being with me now. Please give me ears to hear, and a heart that understands. Show me what You want me to learn about You, and about me.

DAY TWO:

A Heart to Understand

But I trust in your unfailing love;
my heart rejoices in your salvation.
I will sing to the LORD,
For he has been good to me.
—Psalm 13:5-6

Above all else, guard your heart,
for it is the wellspring of life.
—Proverbs 4:23

BEFORE YOU BEGIN:

- Pray. Ask God to quiet your mind and help you listen to His voice.
- Determine to be gut-level honest in your responses.
- Commit yourself to the Lord's healing process for you.

QUESTIONS:

In a continued spirit of reflection and contemplation, ask God to give you ears to hear and a heart to understand. Read back through the daily "NOTICING" sections. Check here when you complete this _____.

1. What did you notice about your physical reactions and feelings through the weeks when reviewing your "Noticing" entries?

2. Did you observe any patterns? Did you see or sense any growth?

3. What pieces still feel undone, unmanaged, or unresolved? Perhaps this would be a good time to unpack them at the feet of the cross before we press forward.

NOTICING:

What physical reactions and feelings did you notice?

PRAYER:

Father, thank You for Your still, small voice reminding me I'm close to Your heart, and always on Your mind.

DAY THREE:
A New Thing

Forget the former things;
do not dwell on the past.
See, I am doing a new thing!
Now it springs up; do you not perceive it?
I am making a way in the desert
and streams in the wasteland.
—Isaiah 43:18-19

"What a message! Confess your sins, worship God,
and get on with your life."
—Robert McGee, *The Search for Significance*

BEFORE YOU BEGIN:

- Pray. Ask God to quiet your mind and help you listen to His voice.
- Determine to be gut-level honest in your responses.
- Commit yourself to the Lord's healing process for you.

QUESTIONS:

1. God is in the process of doing a new thing! What do you sense springing up?

2. Write a second letter to your pre-adoptive self. What would you tell her now?

NOTICING:

What physical reactions and feelings did you notice?

PRAYER:

Help me, Father, get on with my life . . . the full, free, abundant life You died to give me. Help me see Your plan and Your purpose.

DAY FOUR:

Reclaiming Hope!

"The LORD your God is with you,
he is mighty to save.
He will take great delight in you,
he will quiet you with his love,
he will rejoice over you with singing."
—Zephaniah 3:17

BEFORE YOU BEGIN:

- Pray. Ask God to quiet your mind and help you listen to His voice.
- Determine to be gut-level honest in your responses.
- Commit yourself to the Lord's healing process for you.

QUESTIONS:

1. The Lord delights in you, and will be with you throughout your journey. Allow Him to quiet you and rejoice over you with singing. How will this affect how you press forward?

2. What are three take-aways you want to apply from this healing support group?

    a.

    b.

    c.

3. How have you reclaimed hope for your adoption journey? Explain:

4. As we embark on this final day of our journey together, imagine riding in a car with your best friend, the person who knows you best and loves you still. The radio blares as you sing along to favorite oldies. Fast food bags litter the floorboard, but you're feeling good! As the sun's warmth kisses your face and sinks into your soul, you know life doesn't get much better than this. Your shared adventure passed through scary territory. You learned to trust one another more, and your friendship grew. Though you'll share future adventures, you feel reluctant to let this one go. Nearing the final leg of the journey, you crest a hill overlooking a sprawling view of your final destination. As you turn to your friend, this is what you say . . .

5. Write a prayer of response to the Father acknowledging the end of this season, and embracing the next:

And that's about it, friends. Be glad in God!
—Philippians 3:1, MSG

WEEKLY SUMMARY AND MEETING

Insights, Thoughts, Comments, and Questions from Reading and Daily Exercises:

How God met me this week:

Support Group Meeting Notes:

ACKNOWLEDGEMENTS:

I'm so thankful I ended up in a place I didn't belong, so I could be found by Him who led me back into His arms. Those dark days led to light, and the joy of sharing the journey with others whose contributions I remain utterly humbled by:

- My Hope's Promise family—staff members who tolerated my writing absences, and carried on without a hitch. You are awesome!

- The Hope's Promise board extraordinaire, many of whom parent children with challenges. Thank you for your encouragement, friendship, and the generous gift of time.

- Precious adoptive moms who shared their stories over coffee, via email, and through daily encounters, with the prayer others might benefit. They confirmed I wasn't alone!

- Tom, Kyle, Rachel, Jennifer, Carol, Paul, Leslie, and Lisa, who reviewed the manuscript for accuracy, and encouraged me with their kind words and helpful suggestions.

- Carol Selander, counselor and trainer. Thank you for allowing God to use you as an effective tool, and for introducing me to grace.

- Dr. Walter Buenning, under whose tutelage I sat for years, as he trained adoptive families at Hope's Promise about attachment and what happens when love goes away.

- Pastor Paul Lessard, who modeled grace and encouraged me to speak.

- Sherrie Eldridge, co-laborer and mentor. Thank you, my friend.

- The wild, wacky, wonderful ladies of Pilot Groups one and two. Thank you for laughter, tears, stories, encouragement, and prayer. You are my heroes!

- Our prayer team, who continues to undergird this message in prayer.

- Lisa, for your trust in sharing your beautiful mosaic story; and Ashlee, for offering your research and networking skills. You have enriched this book and my life.

- My parents, who taught me to love family, work hard, and always tell the truth. Lessons that continue to serve me well.

- My children, Chad (Melissa), Brooke (Erik), Nick (Jenn), Tyler (Holly), Hope, Sarah, and Abby; and my precious grandchildren. I love you all more than you will ever know.

- . . . and Ray, the love of my life. None of this would make sense without you. I love you.

ABOUT THE AUTHOR

Paula is the founder and former executive director of Hope's Promise, a Colorado-based adoption and orphan-care ministry. Paula served for nearly ten years as a national trainer with the Infant Adoption Training Initiative, and is a founding member of the National Christian Adoption Fellowship. She is a member of the Advanced Writer and Speaker's Association.

Inspired by the adoption of her daughter, Hope, from India, Paula returned to graduate school, as a mother of five, to earn her master's degree in social work. Her heart for adoption led her to orphanages in Nepal, Thailand, Vietnam, Cambodia, Ukraine, Kenya, and Sierra Leone, where she helped place orphaned children into US families.

Hope's Promise also places children through domestic adoption, and provides free pregnancy counseling to women with unintended pregnancies. Under Paula's direction, Hope's Promise expanded to five Colorado locations, and offers a full range of adoption services and training to birth and adoptive families.

Moved by the plight of orphans who would not be adopted, Hope's Promise launched an orphan-care division in 2002. Their mission to reflect God's heart through the lifelong journey of adoption and orphan care now includes indigenous staff in four countries (Nepal, Vietnam, Kenya, and Zimbabwe), overseeing their children's homes, educational sponsorship programs, and providing medical care to nearly 5,000 people each year in rural Vietnam.

Paula and her husband, Ray, delight in their seven children, four by birth and three by adoption. They enjoy their growing number of grandchildren, and live in breathtaking Colorado.

For more information on the adoption and orphan care ministries of Hope's Promise, or to learn how you can become involved, please contact them in one of the following ways:

www.hopespromise.com • adopt@hopespromise.com

If you are interested in having Paula speak at your church or upcoming event, please contact her at:

paulasfreeman@gmail.com

And be sure to visit her website at www.paulafreeman.org

SOURCE LIST

THE JOURNEY BEGINS

1. Foster, Richard J. *Prayer: Finding the Heart's True Home*. (New York: Harper Collins Publisher, 1992), 31.

WEEK 2: EXPECTATIONS AND ADOPTION REALITIES

1. Foster, Richard J. *Prayer: Finding the Heart's True Home*. (New York: Harper Collins Publisher, 1992), 31.

WEEK 4: A PLACE I DIDN'T BELONG

1. Gray, Deborah D. *Attaching in Adoption: Practical Tools for Today's Parents*. (Indianapolis, IN: Perspectives Press, 2002), 98.
2. Krivak, Andrew. *A Long Retreat: in Search of a Religious Life*. (New York: Farrar, Straus and Giroux, 2008).

WEEK 5: HOMEWARD BOUND

1. Cameron, Julia. *The Artist's Way: A Spiritual Path to Higher Creativity*. (New York: Tarcher Putnam Publisher, 1992), 98.
2. Stephens, Dr. Steve and Gray, Alice. *The Worn Out Woman*. (Colorado Springs, CO: Multnomah Books, 2004), 156.

WEEK 6: RIGHT INTO HIS ARMS:

1. Swenson, Richard A. *Margin*. (Colorado Springs, CO: NavPress, 2004), 196, 199.
2. Hauerwas, Stanley and Jean Vanier. *Living Gently in a Violent World*. (Downers Grove, IL: Intervarsity Press, 2008), 92-93.

WEEK 7: SUPPORT SYSTEMS:

1. Hauerwas, Stanley and Jean Vanier. *Living Gently in a Violent World*. (Downers Grove, IL: Intervarsity Press, 2008), 37.

2. Schooler, Jayne E. and Thomas C. Atwood. *The Whole Life Adoption Book.* (Colorado Springs, CO: NavPress, 2008).

3. Forbes, Heather and Sophia F. Dziegielewski. "Issues Facing Adoptive Mothers of Children with Special Needs." *Journal of Social Work*, 2003. Sage Publications. www.beyondconsequences.com/issues.pdf.

4. Smith, Melinda and Robert Segal and Jeanne Segal. "Understanding Stress: Symptoms, Signs, Causes and Effects." Helpguide.org. www.helpguide.org/mental/stress_signs.htm.

5. McGee, Robert S. *The Search for Significance.* Nashville: Thomas Nelson Publishing, 2003.

APPENDIX A:
God Wants to Adopt You

God decided in advance to adopt us into his own family by bringing us to himself through Jesus Christ. This is what he wanted to do, and it gave him great pleasure.
—Ephesians 1:5 NLT

Just as our heart longs for our adopted child to embrace us as their parent, with love and without hesitation, so God longs for us to embrace Him. In the ancient world, people would often adopt a child, primarily a boy, to continue the family line. A high cultural priority was placed on maintaining the strength of the family name and the transfer of assets. In contrast, people of the Jewish tradition at that time, out of a sense of gratitude for how God had provided, would adopt children with a desire to confer all the benefits of their family upon the adoptee. Early Christian families took the idea of blessing the orphan a step further, by gathering children the Greeks had abandoned to die of exposure on hillsides, and raising them as their own.

The verse above was written in the context of these Christian families adopting the unwanted and discarded children from other races and cultures. All were seen as valuable in and of themselves, being created in God's image. We, too, are created in God's image, and are of such value to God, that He looks to adopt us and make us His own, conferring on us all the benefits of being one of His children.

Some of us find ourselves rejecting the love of the father, God, as our children have rejected us. Fearing new hurt, our children resist their deep need for connection and family as a means of protecting their hearts from further wounding. Avoiding a relationship with God—fearing God's rejection and the hurt it would cause—is not uncommon. Believing God would turn away if He knew who we really are, we, like our children, run as far and fast as we can in the opposite direction. However, just as many of us traveled to distant lands to meet and bring our child home, so God, through the action of his Son, Jesus, has gone the distance to ensure we, too, can find and make our home with Him.

Ephesians 1:5 tells us that, before we even knew ourselves and who we were, before we even had a chance to make bad decisions and run, God had already decided He wanted us, wanted to make us part of His family, and it would give Him great pleasure to do so.

The way to God is a simple one. Say in your mind or aloud, *"God, I recognize that, in Your love, You want to be my father, and You want me as Your child. Through Your son, Jesus, I want to be Your child, to be adopted into Your family of love, grace, and forgiveness."*

Next Steps

God showed how much he loved us by sending his one and only
Son into the world so that we might have eternal life through him.
—1 John 4:9 NLT

Just as life changed for your son or daughter when they moved into your home, change is the result of God adopting you into His family. God's family, as you prayed above, is one of love, grace, and forgiveness.

Love

1 John 4:9 tells us that God loved us so much he sent Jesus, His son, to make our adoption possible. The Bible teaches there is a huge break in the relationship between God and people, a break stretching almost from the very beginning of the creation of humans. We are born into this broken relationship, and not only suffer the consequences, but often act out this brokenness, much like our children act out in their relationships with us.

Grace

Jesus mends and heals this broken relationship by His death on the cross. This action, coming solely from God's love for us, is called grace. Many of us loved our children before they ever knew us, and we couldn't wait to bring them home, and so it is with God. God's love and grace go hand in hand.

Forgiveness

The practical effect of God's love being expressed in grace is that we are forgiven for all we have done to contribute to the brokenness in our life and world. Our part in this story is to recognize the break, or sin, and be honest about our part in it and the choices we've made. As we recognize and take ownership for our actions, we turn toward God and the life He has welcomed us into. This turning is called repentance, and is a necessary step toward experiencing full forgiveness. In the Bible, the life He offers is called the eternal, or spiritual, life; a life having a relationship with Jesus at its center. The word eternal is often used, as once this relationship begins, it lasts forever.

This is how we know that we live in him and he in us: He has given us of his Spirit.
—1 John 4:13

Holy Spirit

The moment we accept God's love for us, and admit our participation in the brokenness around us—maybe even rebelling against God—the spirit of Jesus, the Holy Spirit, comes and lives within us. The Holy Spirit has the job of reminding us how much God loves us, and of assuring us we are forgiven. Often, when we first decide for God, our lives don't feel much different than before, and we become discouraged. But the Spirit grows in us, like a little seed blooming into a beautiful flowering plant as, over time, the Spirit works inside us, changing, healing, softening, and warming our hearts to God and the new life He has called us to.

Welcome to the Family!

Coming into God's family is a life-altering decision that will affect all your relationships. At the center of this family is your relationship to Jesus, God's son. The best way to understand and grow in your knowledge of this new life is to read God's word, the Bible, and listen to God as He speaks through His Spirit to you. God also speaks through others in His family. God's family most commonly finds expression most commonly in what is called the "church," or community of faith. Finding a faith community where you can experience God's love, grace, and forgiveness through others on this same journey of being adopted by God is important.

Welcome to the family: welcome home!

Paul Lessard
Senior Pastor
Castle Oaks Covenant Evangelical Church
Castle Rock, Colorado

APPENDIX B:
Confidentiality Agreement

During my participation in *A Place I Didn't Belong: Hope for Adoptive Moms* Support Group, I may learn personal and confidential information about individuals participating or otherwise involved with this Group.

Whether information is available to me through the Group or accidentally, I agree to maintain confidentiality, and not reveal information to any person in or outside the Group while I am a Member of the Group, or at any time in the future when I may no longer be a Member of the Group.

Although good-faith efforts have been taken to preserve confidentiality, the confidentiality of information communicated by and between participants in this forum cannot be guaranteed.

Member Signature: _____ Date: _____

Member Signature: _____ Date: _____

Member Signature: _____ Date: _____

Member Signature: _____ Date: _____

Member Signature: _____ Date: _____

Member Signature: _____ Date: _____

Member Signature: _____ Date: _____

Member Signature: _____ Date: _____

Member Signature: _____ Date: _____

Member Signature: _____ Date: _____

Member Signature: _____ Date: _____

Member Signature: _____ Date: _____

Group Leader: _____ Date: _____

APPENDIX C:

Feeling Wheel

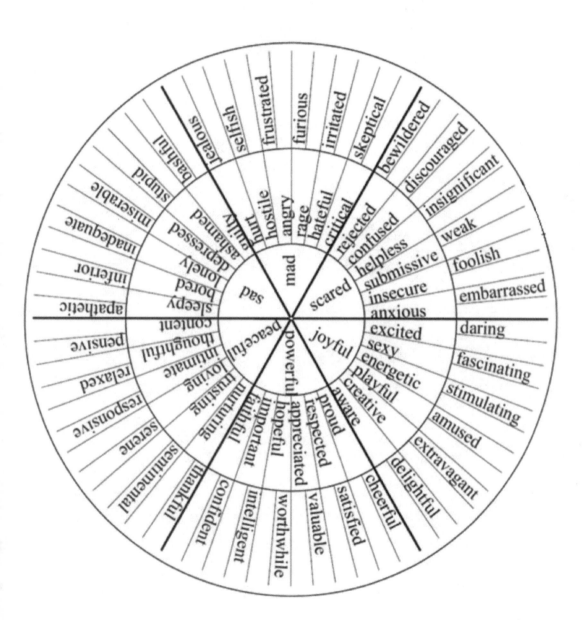

APPENDIX D:
Additional Resources for Your Journey

Ashlee Harry
Adoptive mom, pilot support-group member, and encourager.
Founder, Dark to Dawn

I was in your shoes not long ago. Maybe we're in the same ones now. Really, it would have seemed I was invited to the pilot group of *A Place I Didn't Belong* by chance. But I know better. In the midst of my deep struggle—my family's deep struggle—I found a place of belonging. Paula led the first reading of *A Place I Didn't Belong* in a healing support group she held at Hope's Promise. I joked a few weeks into it that I had waited eight years, and moved 1,800 miles, to find a place of safety among others who intimately understood the condition of my heart. The group was a place of belonging because there are some things you cannot read about—you have to experience them. The common thread was each of us has a child with challenges. And all of us in that first group had an experience allowing us to leave judgment at the door. I felt an unprecedented grace as I shared my pain. I hope each woman felt that same grace lavished upon them. Since then, I have journeyed with a second group of women through Paula's revision of the book. That journey was equally sacred.

Those two groups landed me right where Paula had hoped, and where God intended: in His safe arms. The question I struggled with had been, "is my child going to be OK?" I came wanting this amazing group of women to answer that million dollar question. (Go ahead and giggle here.) But, instead, a different answer came: "You are going to be OK." I will hold onto my faith in Jesus—however the tempest around me blows. I have lived those first few verses of James. The trials I face *are* producing perseverance (James 1:1-2). But, as time has passed, I have come to realize something even greater. Whether or not I hold onto Him, He will never let go of me. His strength is enough for both of us.

Don't misunderstand. This "arrival" is most certainly still in process. And, you ought not arrive in this same spot. No formulas or pat answers exist for our arrival. We have learned all too well that, like our children with challenges, no one-size-fits-all antidotes to our troubles exist. We are each on a unique road. Our commonness is this: we have experienced loss through the deep wounds our children carry. And, more importantly, we are heading toward the same destination: an eternal glory.

Even through pages and across miles, I suspect our hearts are intertwined. Because of my tenderness for your heart's journey, I offer these additional resources, carefully chosen in a spirit of grace, for your continued growth and healing. While each is good, and hand-picked for a variety of reasons, I recognize all may not be appropriate for you. Each resource is reputable, although not all embrace a Christian perspective. I felt it was important to include them and allow you to choose what resonates for you.

I have listed resources to correlate with the major themes in *A Place I Didn't Belong*. In our early pilot groups we found that while one woman wanted to spend weeks on the issues of expectations, another might fly through that, desiring more time on self-care. This resource list is designed to help you in the area where you would like to spend more time.

So, I simply invite you to prayerfully browse through these short summaries, and choose what feels right for you. Some may fit, while others may not. Use these resources in ways to best meet your need. My goal is promoting your wellness by landing safely in His arms.

Grace to you . . .

Ashlee

EXPECTATIONS

Adopted
Barb Lee
www.adoptedthemovie.com

This informative documentary is critical for the adoptive family, while also being uncomfortable. This is a raw tale of adoption stories from two perspectives—one family just starting down the hopeful road of adoption, and the other much further down a tumultuous path. The emotional undercurrents of each person are portrayed to help the viewer gain greater insight into complex nuances of adoption. Core to this video are issues associated with transracial adoption. The stories are told honestly, and each person is respectfully portrayed. From their lives, we glean greater understanding. Companion DVDs are also available, entitled *We Can Do Better.*

Empowered to Connect—Insights: Explore Your Expectations
Dr. Karyn Purvis
www.empoweredtoconnect.org/insights-gifts-video-series/

In the *Gifts and Insights* video series, we are introduced to short videos addressing a wide range of adoption issues. The series includes seven insights and seven gifts, allowing us to dig deeper into the realities we face in adoption. One excellent video explores our expectations in adoption. Dr. Purvis highlights several possibilities of what our expectations may be, and paints a new picture of how we might revise them.

Jen Hatmaker Blog—Fake Family
www.jenhatmaker.com/blog/2011/09/26/fake-family

Jen Hatmaker is a lover of Jesus, and is, consequently, willing to dive deep into the issues of justice. She is authentic and refreshingly imperfect. Her book *Interrupted* recounts the story of leaving a big bustling church ministry to start a church serving in and among the poor. She experiments with reducing our American excess in her book *Seven*. She is a speaker, blogger, pastor's wife, and mother—an adoptive mother. Her blog entries "After the Airport," "How to be the Village," and "Fake Family" went viral in the social media realm. "Fake Family" dispels the myth of the perfect family—whether adoptive or not. Some of us have even wondered how she so poignantly articulated our own ideas and thoughts.

COMPROMISED BEGINNINGS AND CHILDREN WITH CHALLENGES

Attaching in Adoption: Practical Tools for Today's Parents
Deborah D. Gray

All good parents want the best for their children. Secure attachment is core to a child's wellness. In adoption, we have a greater challenge in the arena of attachment, requiring different parenting skills. This book serves as a complete guide, offering education and practical methods to build healthy attachment. Gray has tackled attachment in a careful and objective way, relaying insights despite the fact that attachment theory and research is an evolving science.

The Connected Child: Bring Hope and Healing to Your Ddoptive Family
Karyn Purvis, David Cross, and Wendy Sunshine

This book is one piece of a large and growing repertoire of resources from the Institute of Child Development at Texas Christian University. Truly seeing and understanding the behaviors of children from "hard places" imparts great wisdom. *The Connected Child* describes the needs behind the behaviors of these children—everything from understanding their trauma to brain chemistry changes, sensory processing disorder, attachment, playing with them, and nutrition. *The Connected Child* articulates the variety of needs, and empowers parents with practical skills to help meet them.

Created to Connect: A Christian's Guide to the Connected Child
Dr. Karyn Purvis, Michael & Amy Monroe

This book serves as the companion study guide to *The Connected Child,* and highlights biblical principles that are a foundation for *The Connected Child.* Couples, small groups, or individuals who employ these connecting strategies are the targeted readers.

Empowered to Connect: What Every Adoptive Parent Should Know
Dr. Karyn Purvis
www.empoweredtoconnect.org

This compilation of several short videos provides an overview of children who come from "hard places," and Dr. Purvis's approach to parenting them. This series addresses a wide spectrum, including the truth behind fear in children, sensory processing disorder, giving voice to your child, strategies to connect to your child, and what Dr. Purvis has dubbed the IDEAL response for parents.

The Primal Wound: Understanding the Adopted Child
Nancy Newton Verrier

This book outlines the cornerstone of Verrier's theory: the loss of their birth mother is the core wound people who have been adopted experience. This "primal wound" manifests itself in physical, emotional, psychological, and spiritual ways. The author dissects the lifelong impact of the loss of this first, and primary, relationship. The premise of the "primal wound" launches a careful look at the grief and loss an adoptee experiences, and the behaviors subsequently manifested, such as fear of abandonment, rejection of the adoptive mother, difficulties with trust, and feelings of shame. This theory of the primal wound suggests all adoptees will struggle to varying degrees with the loss of their birth mother. Verrier's discussion of healing, therefore, does not offer many pat answers. But, she does share insights to mitigate this monumental loss. The book addresses everyone in the adoption triad by making a hearty effort to speak to the adoptee, the adoptive parents, and the birth mother/family.

Parenting the Hurt Child: Helping Adoptive Families Heal and Grow
Gregory C. Keck and Regina Kupecky

This is a wonderful book, balancing the critical piece of explaining to parents what is going on inside our hurting children, and strategies to heal them. As we grow in knowledge, they integrate those all too mysterious concepts of how parenting our children can look. Then, of course, they outline parenting techniques that do *not* work. Clearly, there is no simple formula, but this book outlines practical how-to ideas. Included are a variety of resources on therapy for siblings and parents, cultural differences, finances, and marriage. Keck and Kupecky approach adoptive parents with unprecedented grace—something we all need when parenting children with challenges.

The Out-of-Sync Child: Recognizing and Coping with Sensory Processing Disorder
Carol Kranowitz and Lucy Jane Miller

An impoverished sensory environment is all too often an early experience of many adopted children. Early brain development is deeply affected by both positive and negative environmental factors. As a visionary, Kranowitz first published this book defining sensory processing disorder (SPD) in 1998. *The Out-of-Sync Child* has become a parenting handbook and driving force to help define the needs of many children and their parents struggling to find the help they needed. While children with SPD often appear typical, growing research shows there are changes in the brain resulting in difficult behaviors that, if misunderstood, can be extremely frustrating to the child, his or her parents, family, and educators alike. These behaviors can be viewed as a message needing to be understood, rather than simply a behavior to be fixed. This book offers parents an opportunity to see their child through the particular lens of SPD, evaluate whether their child might be manifesting SPD symptoms, and how to obtain effective help.

WOUNDS WE CARRY

Life's Healing Choices: Freedom from Your Hurts, Hang-ups, and Habits
John Baker and Rick Warren

This book is based on the heart of Celebrate Recovery—a Christ-centered recovery program birthed at Saddleback Church. Baker, a pastor at Saddleback, sets the tone by acknowledging we all have hurts, hang-ups, and habits affecting our ability to experience happiness and healing. This book offers eight choices toward healing, based on the Beatitudes of Jesus. Baker addresses grief, pain, crisis, denial, letting go of control, guilt, repairing relationships, and getting help. He gently and truthfully leads us through challenging choices, while being encouraged by the power of a loving God. Scripture illuminates who God is and who we are in Him—enabling us to have confidence to make hard decisions resulting in hope, healing, and happiness.

Parenting From the Inside Out
Daniel Siegel and Mary Hartzell

Founded on the premise that childhood experiences affect how we parent, these authors are quick to argue that even if we experienced troubled childhoods, we need not be defined by them if we gain self-understanding. This book allows us to peek back into influential childhood experiences, and look forward into how we parent our children. *Parenting from the Inside Out* has a sophisticated foundation of science, but weaves throughout stories from which the common reader can grow. Self-study exercises at the end of each chapter allow readers to make this experience personal and therapeutic.

GRACE

The Gifts of Imperfection: Let Go of Who You Think You're Supposed to Be and Embrace Who You Are
Brené Brown

This "Guide to a Wholehearted Life" is founded in Brown's research. But don't be fooled—she is also an incredible storyteller. Featured on PBS, NPR, and TEDx, she tackles several guideposts leading to a life of self-compassion. The book courageously helps the reader cultivate creativity, play, rest, laughter, authenticity, and a resilient spirit. Each guidepost offers antidotes to anxiety, comparison, exhaustion, and the need to feel in control. In an almost surprising fashion, she takes research findings and, through them, offers us a healthy dose of grace. Furthermore, this book gives us a glimpse into vulnerability, the key to building community.

Jen Hatmaker Blog—The Truth About Adoption One Year Later

www.jenhatmaker.com/blog/2012/08/21/the-truth-about-adoption-one-year-later

Jen Hatmaker does it again. Although you and I could copy and paste our own time-line over hers, the spirit of this post leaves us with grace for the journey. Her one year looks a lot like my eighth year. She is both truthful and validating. Grace abounds. This is the story of leaning in—even when it's ugly. But, in the end, if we focus on the main thing, we'll make it, if only by a hair. She reminds us, "In Him we can do this."

GRIEF AND LOSS

Parents with Broken Hearts
William L. Coleman

As a counselor, Coleman has become intimately aware of the struggles parents face. Parenting well is a challenge. If you add the heartache caused by children who have made poor choices into the equation, parents are left with deep hurts in the wake. This book offers wisdom and grace for such parents. A newer edition speaks particularly to adoptive families and their unique challenges. But the universal message is this: in the midst of pain, you can find a place of peace.

Turn My Mourning into Dancing: Finding Hope in Hard Times
Henri Nouwen

This book offers a place of sanctuary for the reader whose heart is aching with grief. Nouwen, who died in 1996, was a Catholic priest, writer, and teacher at some of the most prestigious schools of divinity in the US. He also lived with monks, the poor in Peru, and among the developmentally disabled. His life was characterized by sharing the deep inner workings of his own heart—knowing that what is most personal is also most universal. Nouwen has a gentility in how he walks us through grief toward a genuine hope, trust, faith, and love.

CRISIS, COLLISION, AND EROSION

Shattered Dreams: God's Unexpected Path to Joy
Larry Crabb

This book is unique. Crabb reaches into the heart and soul of pain and suffering. "Life can be tough. It can be tough for sincere Christians who have walked faithfully with Christ for many years." He realistically acknowledges life's difficulties without judgment. How can a God-loving person experience so much hardship? Crabb reminds us God really is good, and will show the reader how. He sends us on a journey toward a better way—a higher way. Not that we shouldn't or won't suffer, but there is a greater end for which we long. "It is a life from God, life with God, life for God." He retells the story of Naomi, from whom God stripped happiness and, subsequently, used her shattered dreams to carry her into a fulfilling life of joy.

One Thankful Mom
My Learning Curve: Restorative Sabbatical
Lisa Qualls
www.onethankfulmom.com

This four-part blog chronicles the journey to restoration for Lisa and Russ Qualls, parents of twelve children through birth and adoption. This passionate wife and mother, who home schooled for twenty years, is an avid blogger; savvy to trauma, attachment, and sensory processing disorder; and advocates for the adoption of HIV+ children. She is incredibly honest and respectful. Her stories tell our stories. In the end, there is one thing tying them together—their faith in Jesus Christ. Qualls also blogs "It Takes a Team" on www.empoweredtoconnect.org.

Where is God?: Finding His Presence, Purpose and Power in Difficult Times
John Townsend

Needless to say, we all have weathered the storms of life. Some are monumental. Other times, a series of smaller storms bombard us. In either case, the haunting question of "Where is God?" may linger. Townsend honestly and gently walks through these questions. He shows that throughout Scripture we find God saying it is OK to ask these hard questions. Townsend turns the reader toward God, causing us to lean into Him. Discover through this book hope, preparedness for the storms ahead, and a fresh energy for life's curves.

BUILDING A HEALTHY COMMUNITY

TED—Ideas Worth Spreading

www.ted.com

Brené Brown: The Power of Vulnerability

Founded in 1984 under the lofty tagline of "ideas worth spreading," TED is a non-profit which based its initial ideas were based in technology, entertainment, and design. It has since become far broader. Among many aspects of TED, one became TEDTalks. TEDTalks provides an avenue to video access of TED conference speakers on the web for a worldwide audience. TEDTalks now includes over 1,000 videos of "ideas worth spreading." Brené Brown talks poignantly about the key aspects of connection with others: vulnerability and authenticity. Before you arrive at connection, however, Brown addresses the reality of shame, fear, control, courage, compassion, and worthiness. This researcher tells universal stories of real people who are finding true connection, love, joy, and creativity.

SPIRITUAL RENEWAL, HEALING, AND SELF-CARE

Jesus Calling

Sarah Young

This daily devotional is a wonderful book to launch your day into close connection with the Savior. Spoken from Jesus's point of view, this book offers great truths lavished in grace. The author, through her own journaling, "hears" what Jesus said to her. Scriptural references support each daily reading, furthering the reader's delight in Scripture. Young's goal is for each reader to experience His presence and His peace. A mobile app also available.

Live a Praying Life

Jennifer Kennedy Dean

To be in prayer is to be connected—in communion—with our Creator. Dean shows that prayer is God's chosen avenue to bind to people, and through prayer, God is moving in power to intervene on earth. While not a formula, this book demonstrates prayer as way of life—a praying life—by being both a study on prayer and a guide to practicing a praying life. Each week she offers new prayer practices, allowing the reader fullness in their relationship with the Savior. The reader is led through five daily readings and prayer practices for thirteen weeks. While its strength may be ushering us into a praying life, Dean also addresses some heart-rending questions. "Why does God not always answer my prayers? Can prayers actually change God's mind?" *Live a Praying Life* is considered by many to be the finest study on prayer.

This is Your Brain on Joy: A Revolutionary Program for Balancing Mood, Restoring Brain Health, and Nuturing Spiritual Growth
Earl Henslin and Dr. Daniel Amen

Did you know all brains are not created equally? Just as early experience shaped the development of our childrens' brains, so, too, have our good and not-so-good experiences in life shaped the way our brains function. Henslin does a refreshing job of explaining how depression, anxiety, anger, attention deficit disorder, post traumatic stress disorder, and the like are not simply spiritual issues. This book marries Christian faith with scientific findings to tell a more complete story of the human experience—particularly when we struggle.

Margin: Restoring Emotional, Physical, Financial, and Time Reserves to Overloaded Lives
Richard A. Swenson MD

Margin identifies and creates restorative solutions for today's overloaded American. Swenson keenly articulates the pains and problems we face. As a clinician, he is uniquely poised to describe the perils of stress we encounter. Swenson first unpacks the problem, and then offers practical insights to rebalance our lives. This book, in the end, is a prescription for health by offering hope. When we create margin, we better navigate tumultuous times, and store up reserves for the unexpected and unwelcome situations life brings.

The Worn Out Woman: When Life is Full and Your Spirit is Empty
Dr. Steve Stephens and Alice Gray

Stephens and Gray lead the reader, step by step, toward recapturing joy. The authors were inspired to write when they learned too many American women feel overwhelmed, over-committed, and as though they have lost something central to themselves. Key topics include guilt, perfectionism, unrealistic expectations, shattered dreams, friendship, and forgiveness. This book attempts to offer a new era characterized by healthy ways of managing the complexities of life, while maintaining a full heart. The simple and practical steps remain under girded by the gracious support worn-out women truly need.

FORGIVENESS

Angie Washington Blog: Forgiveness: A Synonym for Adoption

http://www.angiewashington.com/2011/04/forgiveness-a-synonym-for-adoption/

The issues that demand forgiveness could cover hurts and history so wide we could never catalogue them all. We all experience relationships where, under the best of intentions, hurts resulted. We experienced these wounds before we became parents, and since. One blogger, Angie Washington, writes an adoptive mother's litany of wounds requiring forgiveness. This choice to forgive, however, does not come easily. She writes, "There are times I choose to turn my back on what could be the sorrowful path to a freer heart." When she musters the gumption to "labor" toward freedom, the spirit of forgiveness this mother doles out might uncover for us an area of hurt we didn't even know existed. But these "overturned rocks" might just open the door to a refreshing peace.

Total Forgiveness
R.T. Kendall

Under the microscope, this book defines what forgiveness is and what it is not. Freedom lies on both sides of these definitions. Kendall rebuts the old adage "forgive and forget" through this wise counsel: "It is actually a demonstration of great grace when we are fully aware of what occurred—and we still choose to forgive." Tucked into this rich book lies the huge subject of self-forgiveness, which could be life-giving for adoptive parents who kick themselves over things they didn't know or might have done. While this book follows lessons from Kendall's personal process through choosing and practicing forgiveness, the highlighted biblical truths throughout are foundational.

MARRIAGE SUPPORT

The Five Love Languages: The Secret to Love that Lasts
Gary D. Chapman

The Five Love Languages is a classic for understanding how to love your spouse. Years of counseling informed Dr. Chapman's classification of five love languages through which people express and interpret life. They are: words of affirmation, quality time, receiving gifts, acts of service, and physical touch. Once you identify your spouse's love language, you are able to express your love for them in a way they can appreciate and receive. Dr. Chapman's wisdom does not stop there. His other books include *Five Love Languages for Children*, *Five Love Languages for Teens*, *Five Love Languages of Apology*, *Desperate Marriage*, and more.

Love & Respect: The Love She Most Desires;
The Respect He Desperately Needs
Emerson Eggerichs

Dr. Eggerichs unpacks a deep mystery of marriage: husbands need to feel respected, and wives need to feel loved. This simple truth, however, has proven far more difficult than it would seem. This book addresses a wide range of scenarios, including marital crisis, loneliness in marriage, engaged couples, and victims of affairs. Founded on biblical principles, Emerson shares real-life tales with which the reader can relate, using them to describe foundations for building a healthier marriage. *Love and Respect* conferences and small group DVD series are also available at www.loveandrespect.com.

Love and War: Find Your Way to Something Beautiful in Your Marriage
John Eldredge and Stasi Eldredge

Some believe *Love and War* is the best Eldredge book yet. In keeping with the spirit of *Wild at Heart* and *Captivating*, this book reminds us not only are we part of a bigger story, our marriages are, too. Marriage is part of God's story, a love story set in the midst of a real war. The authors quickly point out our first shock in marriage is that it is hard, and the second, which comes swiftly on the heels of the first, is that both husband and wife are a "royal mess." Their authentic portrayal of marital challenges offers relief in the commonness of the marriage experience. Their success in maneuvering these trying times leaves us yearning for the full beauty of marriage. Companionship, finding the mission for your marriage, prayer, and sex are discussed. The chapter entitled "The Little Foxes" describes warfare, and how to ensure your marriage is nothing short of fantastic. They lead us into the ways marriage "can be done," and reassure us it is "worth it."

Weekend to Remember
www.familylife.com

Founded upon biblical foundations and time-tested principles, Family Life offers weekend marriage conferences throughout the United States. They help couples strengthen their marriages.

PARENTING CHILDREN WITH CHALLENGES

20 Things Adoptive Kids Wish their Adoptive Parents Knew
Sherrie Eldridge

This book, written by an adult adoptee with a profound understanding of the inner workings of the adopted child, does a beautiful and respectful job of giving voice to children who have been adopted. She unravels twenty complex emotional issues invaluable for adoptive parents to understand. While these truths can sometimes be hard to swallow, they are no less true. One, for example, is a child's need for parents to talk about their birth family. At first, this can feel like climbing a mountain, but doing so regularly allows parents to help their child talk about what she is already thinking. Our children need help to process grief and loss, and to develop trust in order to lay the groundwork for a bright future. We have an enormous responsibility and privilege in ushering them into healthy adulthood, but at the core of parenting these children is seeing the world through their eyes, thereby helping mend their hurts.

20 Things Adoptive Parents Need to Succeed
Sherrie Eldridge

Eldridge tackles the topic of adoptive parenthood, which lies outside her specific experience, with uncanny understanding. This is a woman who, as an adoptee, made it her life work to gain wellness for herself. With that wholeness, she has become a most gracious and careful listener. Understanding all perspectives in the adoption triad, she has seen into the heart of adoptive parents. Growing up as an adoptee offers great insight into our role as parents. She integrates vignettes into each chapter. These give voice to what our children need, and offers adoptive parents hope for connection to our children in a tender parent-child relationship. Eldridge is a truth-teller with heaps of kindness and grace. She speaks to the challenging reality our children face, while bolstering our parental hearts. This is a must read, not only for understanding, but for encouragement. Included in this book are Support Group Discussion Questions for those reading it together in community.

Adoption Parenting: Creating a Toolbox, Building Connections
Jean MacLeod and Sheena Macrae, Editors

This A to Z book on adoption was born through a Yahoo! group aptly called Adoption Parenting. Over one hundred contributors, with editing expertise by Jean MacLeod and Sheena Macrae, address every adoption topic under the sun. When you feel concerned about your child's sleep, food, language, attachment issues, discipline, loss and grief, school, race, parent support, and sibling issues, this book serves as a quick reference. Or, shelve it for another season, to be read again for wisdom and guidance in the next step of the adoption journey.

Jean MacLeod
www.adoptiontoolbox.com

This comprehensive website will link you to numerous resources. MacLeod is a living testimony, as mother of three adopted daughters.

Trust-Based Parenting: Creating Lasting Changes in Your Child's Behavior
DVD available from www.child.tcu.edu

Produced by the Institute of Child Development at Texas Christian University, this DVD is based on ten years of research forming the basis for the therapeutic approach called Trust-Based Relational Intervention (TBRI). Dr. Karyn Purvis and Dr. David Cross are developmental psychologists who demonstrate strategies for working with children from "hard places." These real-life scenarios offer practical ways to parent children with challenges, using core principles of TBRI—Empowering, Connecting, and Correcting.

SEEKING PROFESSIONAL HELP

Choosing medical or professional help for you, your child, and your family is not easy. Children may require varied assessments and therapies. Parents may visit four, five, six, or more professionals before landing with one they believe can help. But take heart! The community of medical professionals is growing both in wisdom and their ability to help. A number of specialty clinics and therapeutic approaches now exist across the nation which may help your child and your family. While this is not an exhaustive list, it offers a starting point to seek additional care you or your child may need. Having been down this road, we want to offer a few tips to help you choose the right professional for you and your family:

- Ask other adoptive families you know who they see and why. Ask them about the guiding principles of the therapist or therapeutic approach. Ask how the professional has proven helpful.
- Interview the professional from whom you are seeking help. Ask questions (see below) to gain a better understanding of their therapeutic approach.
- Trust your gut. While one therapy might work for one child or family, a different therapeutic approach may be a better fit for your family.
- Parents should be an integral part of the treatment team. The goal is for the child to find safety with primary caregivers. Primary caregivers must be central to the attachment and healing for a child, and should be present in therapy. If the therapist wants to work only with issues surrounding the child, then relationships cannot be healed. Attachment-challenged children have relational hurts, so everyone in the family needs to develop relational skills—especially children.
- Be wary of professionals who purport to have a 100 percent success rate. No quick fixes or formulas to help children with trauma and attachment challenges exist.
- Be wary of a professional who judges or misjudges parents for the child's behavior.
- Choose a professional who understands the family as a whole has been affected by the challenging child(ren). The needs and wellness of the entire family are important. A professional caring for you as a parent, or other children in the family, can have a monumental impact on the child with challenges.

Potential Therapeutic and Medical Resources:

American Academy of Pediatrics—Council on Foster Care, Adoption,
and Kinship Care
www2.aap.org/sections/adoption/index.html

ATTACh—Association for Treatment and Training in the Attachment of Children
www.attach.org

Attachment and Bonding Center of Ohio—Dr. Gregory Keck
www.abcofohio.net

C.A.S.E. Center for Adoption Support and Education
www.adoptionsupport.org

Center for Adoption Medicine—University of Washington
www.adoptmed.org

Children's Research Triangle
www.childstudy.org

Child Trauma Academy
www.childtrauma.org

Jane Aronson, MD
www.orphandoctor.com

Inward Bound Colorado—Jennifer Winkelmann MA, LPC, NCC
www.inwardboundco.com

North American Council on Adoptable Children
www.nacac.org

University of Alabama
www.adoption.childrensal.org

University of Chicago
www.uchicagokidshospital.org

University of Minnesota—Dana Johnson MD
www.peds.umn.edu/iac

Questions to Help You Choose the Right Therapist

1. Interview a few therapists—even a handful—before you choose one.

2. How long is the therapist willing to work with your family? Working with kids who have experienced trauma is a long process, requiring enduring support.

3. The therapist must understand preverbal trauma, the adoptive process, the adoptive child, and the adoptive family. Ask about their experience in these areas. How many families have they worked with, and for how long?

4. They must understand emotional regulation, attachment, early development, and the development of empathy on a neurophysiological level. Ask them to explain one of these concepts to you as a part of the interview.

5. Will the therapist work with you *and* your child? Or, will the therapist work only with you—the parents?

6. What system of support does the therapist have? These mental health professionals need their own support system, because their work is emotionally draining. As your go-to professional, the therapist you choose needs to be well and whole while supporting you.

7. Ask the therapist why they do this work. This will help you learn about the person who may enter into the inner circle of your family.

Key Characteristics of a Therapist:

- compassionate
- non-judgmental
- have done work of their own, dealing with their own struggle
- creative
- up to date on current research and literature
- collaborative with other professionals

Source: *The Right Fit—Finding Effective Help for Families with Attachment Challenged Children, Inward Bound, 2008.*

OTHER RESOURCES

Adoptive Family Magazine

www.adoptivefamilies.com

This nationally-recognized resource addresses all aspects of adoption: pre-placement, the wait, long after the arrival of your child, open adoption, transracial adoption, and international adoption. This resource is helpful in both the print format and as an online resource.

Empowered to Connect

www.empoweredtoconnect.org

This website provides relevant information covering a wide range of topics from trauma, loss and grief, family and friends, and sensory processing disorder to trauma and brain chemistry. Several short videos covering these topics, and others, are included.

Joint Council on International Children's Services

www.jointcouncil.org

This non-profit, non-governmental organization's mission to "advance the overall well-being of vulnerable children and their right to live in permanent family care," serves orphans and vulnerable children in fifty-three countries, including the US.

North American Council on Adoptable Children

www.nacac.org

Founded on the principle that all waiting children need loving families, and post-adoption support is critical to the success of children and their families, this resource addresses a wide range of physical, emotional, and mental needs both of children who have been adopted and their adoptive families.

National Council for Adoption

www.adoptioncouncil.org

This non-profit advocates for adoption and promotes a culture of adoption through education, research, and legislative action. NCFA focuses on infant adoption, adoption out of foster care, and international adoption.

Tapestry Books

www.tapestrybooks.com

The first of its kind, Tapestry Books specializes in a wide array of adoption books and resources. This is a great source for adoption-appropriate books for children, adoption life books, parenting books, the adoption triad, and pre-adoption books.

The Theraplay Institute

www.theraplay.org

Theraplay is a family-based therapy model using four core concepts: structure, nurture, engagement, and challenge. Intended to create healthy attachments, self-esteem, and relational skills, Theraplay specializes in helping children with a wide range of social, emotional, developmental, and behavioral challenges. Theraplay trained professionals are available throughout the US and abroad. Books and video resources are also available through this website.

The Post Institute

www.thepostinstitute.com

Bryan Post, founder of The Post Institute, was adopted out of the foster care system. His life experience led him to a career helping families who have children with numerous disorders leading to difficult behaviors. His Stress Model is a love-based approach to parenting children with challenges. The website is packed with resources that can be ordered or downloaded—some for free. The Post Institute offers therapy, camps, seminar trainings, and webinars.

John Piper: What Does it Mean to Live by Faith in the Service of the Fatherless?
Recorded at the Orphan Summit April 30, 2010
http://www.desiringgod.org/resource-library/conference-messages/what-does-it-mean-to-live-by-faith-in-the-service-of-the-fatherless

This sermon might be one of the finest on the topic of adoption. Piper preaches not so much about the biblical mandate to adopt, but what life could hold when we do adopt. Piper reminds us of the war we wage as adoptive families, and that we are part of an eternal story.

APPENDIX E:

Stepping Stones of Hope
The Mosaic Experience
A Metaphor of Renewal and God's Grace

Lisa Eisenhardt
baytobison@live.com
www.piecefullymade.com
© 2012 used by permission

WELCOME TO A PLACE YOU BELONG

Hi Sisters,

I know you! At the very least, we have something in common. We are searching for hope—real and lasting hope—and love, to give us strength in our adoption journeys. I searched for support in obvious places for almost four years. Friends, family, and counselors who didn't have the same experiences I had just couldn't understand.

Books and programs gave fleeting comfort.

When I started *A Place I Didn't Belong* with Paula, and a dozen or so other women I'd never met, I had no expectations. I was ready to try again out of desperation. Less than an hour into our first discussion, it was apparent these women knew me. They truly empathized with my situation. Their tears and stories held wisdom and lifted me up. I still didn't know where I was going, but I knew I was going somewhere. I belonged *there*.

A SEED IS PLANTED

I loved the little seaside town we were exploring, and soaked it all in. I did not expect a seed to be planted in my heart that day. A seed to last a lifetime. I walked toward the shop, navigating around objects such as an old column from a front porch, a wagon, and a door frame. I was captivated by them because they were so imperfect, yet all so unique and beautiful. All had been painstakingly covered with stones, coins, shards of glass, and ceramics in random patterns. I wanted to try this—and, soon, I started making mosaic stepping stones. Once I started making stepping stones, I soon had a whole path of them. Making those stepping stones was cathartic and healing. God was showing me His redeeming, transforming, and healing power. He revealed a metaphor to me: my life, although shattered, fragmented, and broken, was becoming beautiful.

While completing *A Place I Didn't Belong,* I felt led to approach and share my experience with Paula. We agreed including a mosaic art project with each support group would be a wonderful way to further bond our incredible community of women. The following stories, injected into the process of making a mosaic stepping stone, come from different times in my life. I pray you will have the same freedom given to you that I gained through this group experience. I now know I can be OK, even when my child is not. Hope is in my home again.

With love,

Lisa

THE PLATE

The unbroken plate represents our life as we had hoped it we would be—no cracks and no missing pieces—whole and complete. The plate could also represent our hearts.

BROKENNESS

I spotted the untidy house while traveling an equally untidy dirt road flooded with overgrown vegetation on either side. The mess encouraged me, because there could be loads of junk. The pungent aroma of Eucalyptus trees nearly overcame me as I moved toward the massive tables layered with treasures. Spotting a stack of plates, I stopped to examine them. "Make an offer," said the woman nearby. Accepting my offer of eight dollars, she began wrapping up the plates. I told her not to bother, because I was just going to hammer them into pieces later, anyway. "These were my aunt's! I'm not gonna sell them to you, then," she snapped. I wondered why she cared? Explaining I planned to make mosaic stepping stones with the plates did not change her mind; the proprietor of the garage sale was not giving them up to me. I left empty-handed. That woman did not understand how beautiful brokenness can be, but I did.

My life had been broken apart by painful childhood events, divorce, drug and alcohol abuse, rejection, promiscuity, veiled suicide attempts, loneliness, and more. Many pieces were left behind. Later in life, I adopted a traumatized child, and the brokenness continued.

THE HAMMER

The hammer represents anything breaking our life apart, such as adoption realities. When the hammer hits your plate, you may not wind up with as many fragments as I had, but we are all broken from one or more events in our lives. Left alone, these fragments are sharp and dangerous. They can wound us and others, or reopen old wounds. Without a buffer between them, they will rub together, causing friction, and eventually erode the pieces away.

Wrap your plate in an old towel, flip it upside down, put your gloves and safety glasses on, and enjoy breaking the plate! With each crash of the hammer, name an assault. Be careful to not let the fragments fly all over the place. Lift up the towel to see what you have, and if you want more pieces, hammer some more. You want flat pieces. After everyone has finished breaking their plates, put all the pieces into one container. What a beautiful mess! This is our "community" (if you're doing this in a group).

DENIAL

Living in Los Angeles in the 80s, I was doing well by the world's standards. I dressed in my facade every day; it seemed I was fooling everyone, including myself. I had chosen a very stressful career, and really looked forward to cocktails with my colleagues after work, then wine at home by myself. I was painfully lonely, and unsatisfied with my job. My life was a raging wind, swirling up around me, yet I took no shelter. In that wind, the debris and pain of my past was like sand in my eyes, obscuring my vision. I was carrying around the fragments of my life. I held on tight. I wanted to give them up, but didn't know what to do with them. I was in denial.

SHATTERED LIVES

Our human nature causes us to want to control and fix everything on our own. Our tendency might be to embrace denial, leaving the fragments in a pile. Or, perhaps we decide to glue the pieces back together, trying to make the plate look as it originally had, which is not possible. Even if you *could* glue the plate back together, it wouldn't look the same. And, if you ever dropped it, your plate could shatter into even more fragments.

Friends, there is no way to put this old plate back together. We have to let our Creator make something new out of our fragments. We can't do this on our own.

But the pot he was shaping from the clay was marred in his hands; so the potter
formed it into another pot, shaping it as seemed best to him.
—Jeremiah 18:4

Do not conform any longer to the pattern of this world, but be transformed
by the renewing of your mind. Then you will be able to test and approve what
God's will is—his good, pleasing and perfect will.
—Romans 12:2

THE STONE

We need a foundation upon which to build our lives. Not a foundation of our own making, based on flawed human direction, flimsy dreams, and self-control, but a firm foundation. The stone represents the foundation we need—Jesus Christ. Feel how solid and heavy the stone is. The stone can carry the weight of all our brokenness!

MOVING OUT OF DENIAL

My most awful moment became my finest, when God found me mired in a dark pit with nowhere to look but up. I had tried long enough using my own strength, my own controls, and my own life systems. I didn't know Him. I stumbled my way onto a different path, taking all my defects with me. He opened His accepting arms wide to embrace me. Broken, confused, angry, and hurt, I surrendered my life to Jesus Christ. I have laid down many fragments since then, and will continue to do so. He is my rock and redeemer. My circumstances change, and are sometimes difficult, but He remains the same.

For no one can lay any foundation other than the one already laid, which is Jesus Christ.
—1 Corinthians 3:11

As you come to him, the living Stone—rejected by men but chosen by God and precious to him—you also, like living stones, are being built into a spiritual house to be a holy priesthood, offering spiritual sacrifices acceptable to God through Jesus Christ. For in Scripture it says:
"See, I lay a stone in Zion,
a chosen and precious cornerstone,
and the one who trusts in him
will never be put to shame."
—1 Peter 2:4-6

MORTAR

The mortar adheres the fragments to the stone. My salvation is represented by the mortar. If God hadn't found me in the pit of despair, where I eventually repented and accepted Him as the leader of my life, I wouldn't have Him as my Savior. I would have nowhere to place my broken pieces. I know now that I am forgiven. I will continue to ask for forgiveness whenever I need it. Remember, this is a process. We're not saved one minute, and everything is perfect the next. This path we're on is for the rest of our lives. Mortar takes time to cure, as well. Leave it to dry for a few days before applying grout.

INTO MY FATHER'S ARMS

Her eyes held a darkness I hadn't seen before in a child, and they were focused on me. I felt scared and afraid of a little girl. Her threats seemed real, and I didn't know how to respond; I was emotional, and everything spiraled out of control. All the books I had read became irrelevant. This was different; it was happening to me. Her words sliced me open, my soul spilling out in front of her. My upwelling despair and fear was familiar, and I reacted with anger at her ripping away the curtain that had covered my fear and anguish as a child. I fell apart, into many pieces.

My weakness eventually turned into my strength. I learned to face her sufferings in ways that wouldn't tear me down over and over. I don't always know why I have another fragment of my life to give to God, or what it really means, but I always know where to lay it down.

Mix the mortar according to the directions. Using a plastic knife, "butter" a fragment and place it on the stone. You're on the way to a new creation! Keep using this technique until the top of the stone is complete. You will want to leave an approximate one-eighth-inch gap between each fragment, where the grout will be placed.

GROUT

We have placed the fragments (our broken hearts, shattered dreams—our very lives), on the living stone. Now the gaps in between the fragments need to be filled. Our salvation is solid, but we need to return to the throne every day for His endless mercy and grace. As I put the grout on my stone, I imagine it represents God's grace and mercy, filling in those gaps when I feel defeated and in despair, or waiting for the other shoe to drop. The grout is what turns our stepping stone into a work of art. Metaphorically, it binds the fragments into a pattern designed by God, not one of our own making. The end result might not be what we expected, but it is His design. Our life, once a messy pile of fragments, now becomes a thing of beauty.

WAITING IN THE GAP

Four years into our adoption and she's still doing this? I can't believe we are in this place again. In my mind, the last thing I want to do is hold her in my arms and wipe away her tears. Her glares and venomous words still sting, but something's different—I have a confidence only God could give me. I am calm. I am OK. She isn't, but I am. This separation gives me the strength to help her one more time. At the end of the day, I pick up the pieces from the damage she has done, and take them to the cross. This day is over now, and there will be new mercies tomorrow.

The next step is messy, so have a plastic tarp ready. Mix the grout, and prepare a bucket of water for rinsing the sponges. Apply the grout with a spatula, working it in between the fragments. Next, wet a sponge, wring it out, and wipe off the excess grout, repeating this step as many times as you need. Also grout the sides where fragments meet the stone. Imagine God's healing power wiping our messy lives clean as you do this.

Let us then approach the throne of grace with confidence, so that we may receive
mercy and find grace to help us in our time of need.
—Hebrews 4:16

SEALANT

The process continues. After the grout has dried, you are ready to apply grout sealant. The sealant represents hope and the Holy Spirit. Our stones may look finished. We could put them in our gardens and hope the elements don't destroy them. But, if the grout isn't sealed, our mosaics will begin cracking, and eventually the fragments will fall off the stone. Our hope doesn't rest in platitudes like "try this and hope it works," or "time heals all wounds." Our hope is a different kind of hope: it comes from the truth of God. Our hope is everlasting, and cannot be penetrated by any circumstance or pain. We may suffer through many storms, but the Holy Spirit will always be in us.

Turn the sealant bottle upside down and squeeze the sealer onto the grouted areas until fully saturated. Wait for the sealant to dry, and then apply again until you notice sealant beading up on the surface of the stone. This indicates the stone is fully sealed and ready for the next storm.

Not only so, but we also rejoice in our sufferings, because we know that
suffering produces perseverance; perseverance, character; and character, hope.
And hope does not disappoint us, because God has poured out his love into our
hearts by the Holy Spirit, whom he has given us.
—Romans 5:3-5

And you also were included in Christ when you heard the word of truth,
the gospel of your salvation. Having believed, you were marked in
him with a seal, the promised Holy Spirit,
—Ephesians 1:13

DISPLAYING HIS SPLENDOR

Where do we go from here? Take your beautiful **new creation** and put it out for all to see. We can be examples for all people living without hope. Our journeys hold tremendous transformational power, not only to us as individuals, but also to the community around us. As we continue piecing together the spiritual meaning from our experiences, and further engage with God on our journey, keep in mind what we want to perpetuate. More isolation, lack of understanding, and judgment? Of course not! Each time you look at your stepping stone, remember that some of those broken pieces belong to your sisters. We need to help each other carry our burdens. Continue to lift each other up in prayer, and rejoice. We are a unique community. No one else truly understands the intensity, heartache, demands, and joys we experience. The uniqueness of our journeys allow us to have far-reaching impact. Together, through the renewing of our minds, we are examples of Christ-like love. The racist neighbor may change her mind after witnessing your love for your child. A church leader may become educated in the world of post-adoption family needs. A family member may get to the core of their own hurts through your experience. However, we cannot do this alone. We need each other. Share your story. Be the first stepping stone on a path for someone to leave "a place they didn't belong," and go back into their Father's arms.

Therefore, if anyone is in Christ, he is a new creation;
the old has gone, the new has come!
—2 Corinthians 5:17

-to bestow on them a crown of beauty instead of ashes, the oil of gladness
instead of mourning, and a garment of praise instead of a spirit of despair.
They will be called oaks of righteousness, a planting of the LORD
for the display of his splendor.
—Isaiah 61:3